STRATEGIC BUDGETING

STRATEGIC BUDGETING

A Comparison Between U.S. and Japanese Companies

Akira Ishikawa

PRAEGER SPECIAL STUDIES • PRAEGER SCIENTIFIC

New York • Philadelphia • Eastbourne, UK
Toronto • Hong Kong • Tokyo • Sydney

Library of Congress Cataloging in Publication Data

Ishikawa, Akira, Data
  Strategic Budgeting

  Includes index.
  1. Budget in business—Case studies.   2. Corporations—Japan—Finance—
Planning—Case studies.   3. Corporations—United States—Finance—Planning—
Case studies.   4. Corporate planning—Japan—Case studies.   4. Corporate plan-
ning—United States—Case studies.   I. Title.
HG4028.B8184   1985   658.1'54   84-18037
ISBN 0-03-071852-X (alk. paper)

Published in 1985 by Praeger Publishers·
CBS Educational and Professional Publishing
a Division of CBS Inc.
521 Fifth Avenue, New York, NY 10175 USA
© 1985 by Praeger Publishers

456789 052 987654321

Printed in the United States of America
on acid-free paper

Preface

It goes without saying that resource allocation issues are so inextricably intertwined with the jobs in any organization, as well as with our daily lives, that even a slightly innovative idea or approach can be of great benefit, and can even change our futures dramatically.

For example, if President Franklin D. Roosevelt had failed to allocate funds for the research and development of the atom bomb, in response to Dr. Albert Einstein's suggestion in 1939, and if a group of German scientists under the control of the Nazis had received an adequate allocation of funds and had developed the same bomb in the early 1940s, human history would have been completely different.

The same is true in the automobile industry. If Chrysler, Ford, and General Motors could have anticipated rising gasoline prices and reallocated their resources to develop the production of small cars, they would have not experienced the problems with which they are still struggling.

In our own lives, we spend a lot of time regretting our failure to allocate our resources to the right places at the right times. If we had only bought that house five years earlier, when mortgage rates weren't so high, or if John could have had the advantage of a background of artificial intelligence, or if Mary could have made a trip to Japan in 1975 . . . . All these resource allocations have immeasurable effects on the rest of our lives.

Although planning is by no means a panacea, there are no other alternatives if we are to minimize the intensity of possible future regrets. As we seek to perfect our planning, we progress from daily planning to weekly planning and to annual planning. Experience has shown that the longer the period of the plan becomes, the better the future we create for ourselves.

Regardless of either our orgnizational or our personal lives, strategic planning is the best intellectual activity that will enable us to perfect our accomplishments as responsible individuals. If there are no aims or objectives in our private or organizational lives, then no strategic planning can be valid. However, if we believe that the rationale of our existence, as well as that of our organization, rests on perfecting truth, virtue, and beauty, then strategic planning will be important.

However, strategic planning alone cannot accomplish this formidable task. In order to improve strategic planning, once it is established, we clearly require budgetary control. Thus, strategic budgeting should be the activity in which we focus. Once we identify strategic planning as an in-depth, resource-allocation activity supported by quantitative information, we can evaluate more objectively and equitably the manner in which we allocate our limited resources.

Based on this viewpoint, this book consists of two parts: establishing the strategic budget and effectuating it. The first part covers mainly the fundamentals, contents, implementation and enhancement of strategic planning, including the contents, implementation and enhancement of strategic planning, including the definition of key terms. Toward the end of this part, the linkage of strategic planning with budgeting becomes more and more highlighted.

The second part deals with how to effectively introduce, manage, and enhance strategic budgeting. In order to streamline the introducton of strategic budgeting, cross-impact analysis is defined, its role clarified, and its future directions illustrated with case histories.

In addition, Chapter 7 is devoted to case studies, one of which is the case of ABC International, which also appears throughout the book as an illustration of a point or concept. The other two cases are quite realistic and may be applied to almost any company in many respects.

This book will be of value to executives, managers (especially corporate managers), administrators, budget specialists, controllers, accountants, and management science specialists in the private sector. It will also be of great interest to administrators and planning, budgeting and analysis officials and staffs in the public sector. In addition, this book can be used as a text in the areas of accounting, budgeting, and management, including strategic planning and management and policy analysis.

I am indebted to many people for their help in preparing this manuscript. Mr. Peter Pyhrr's work on zero-base budgeting has provided me with a solid foundation; it is based on Dr. David Novick's work on program budgeting of 1965, on which the concept and technique of strategic budgeting have gradually grown up My thanks also go to Dr. Sidney Shoeffler, who generously allowed me to use the case of Apollo Industries, and to John O'Shea, who took on the painstaking job of polishing my Japanese English. Kenneth Gentner, one of my former students, contributed greatly to preparing Chapter 8. Lorraine Kenny and her word-processing equipment have been of immense assistance in avoiding what otherwise would have been a far more repetitive job.

Akira Ishikawa
February 1984

Contents

List of Tables

List of Figures

STRATEGIC BUDGETING

Introduction

—1—

In the course of human history, some 20 civilizations have risen and fallen. Of these, a few have lasted long and achieved much; others fell soon and were forgotten.

The search for reasons that explain these changes leads quickly to one failing common to all: the lack of foresight by a ruler or administrator—the failure to perceive in which direction the events of an era were heading, and what the consequences would be if no planned action were taken.

Thus, the vital factor is planning—or, to use a term popular in business and public administration, "strategic planning," which applies to civilizations as well as to corporations. A current example of the inability to plan properly is described by two students of current business practices:

> What emerges from our analysis is the failure on the part of U.S. companies to think strategically in global terms. Relative strategic advantages that appear, due to currency devaluation or energy price hikes, have not been seized. The orientation is domestic, short term, and ultimately fatal.[1]

There is little doubt that the economic dominance of U.S. companies will continue to weaken as long as management and labor continue to cling to the orientations that have characterized them in the past. For three specific examples of this narrow-minded view, we have only to look at steel in the United States, faced with international competition rather than domestic competition, the results only too evident; the business-government relationship in the United States, which has become more adversary rather than more cooperative; and the continuing criterion of short-term dollar return rather than enhancement of corporate development as the measure of success.

For business to survive and prosper in the 1980s and 1990s, the importance of strategic planning, supported by a well-designed resource allocation and reallocation system, cannot be overstressed.

In the following sections I intend to define the place of strategic planning in the organization of management, to identify external and internal constraints, and to demonstrate the inevitable necessity of strategic, planning-oriented budgeting.

1

THE PLACE OF STRATEGIC PLANNING IN MANAGEMENT

In their "Ten Commandments of Management," Ross and Kami have shown the importance they attach to strategic planning by placing it first:

I. Develop and communicate a strategy, a unified sense of direction to which all members of the organization can relate.

II. If you want to achieve plans, programs and policies, then overall controls and cost controls must be established.

III. Exercise care in the selection of a board of directors and require that they actively participate in management.

IV. Avoid one-man rule.

V. Provide management depth.

VI. Keep informed of change, and react to change.

VII. Don't overlook the customer and the customer's new power.

VIII. Use but don't misuse computers.

IX. Do not engage in accounting manipulations.

X. Provide for an organizational structure that meets the needs of the people.[2]

They continue, "To develop and communicate a strategy, a unified sense of direction to which all members of the organization can relate is probably the most important concept in management, yet it is frequently overlooked."[3] They caution, however, that "Such platitudes as 'make a profit' or 'increase market share' do not provide the unified direction we are seeking."[4]

Even though Ross and Kami have captured the essence of strategic planning and properly stressed its importance, their discussion of it is confined to general terms. Far more specific definitions are offered by other commentators. One study sees strategy as the main identifying characteristic of the company:

> For us, strategy is the pattern of objectives, purposes or goals, and major policies and plans for achieving these goals, stated in such a way as to define what business the company is in or is to be in and the kind of company it is or is to be.[5]

Another defines strategy in terms of strategic planning, as compared with management control and operational control:

> Strategic planning is the process of deciding on objectives of the organization, on changes in these objectives, on the resources used to attain these ojectives, and on the policies that are to govern the acquisition, use and disposition of these resources.

Management control is the process by which managers assure that resources are obtained and used effectively and efficiently in the accomplishment of the organization's objectives.

Operational control is the process of assuring that specific tasks are carried out effectively and efficiently.[6]

Thus, while one definition sees strategy as a part of objectives, purposes, and goals, another ties it to both objective identification and resource allocation. Another definition incorporates both of these, and adds more:

The strategy of an organization, or of a sub-unit of a larger organization, is a conceptualization, expressed or implied by the organization's leader, of (1) the long-term objectives or purposes of the organization, (2) the broad constraints and policies, either self-imposed by the leader or accepted by him from his superiors, that currently restrict the scope of the organization's activities, and (3) the current set of plans and near-term goals that have been adopted in the expectation of contributing to the achievement of the organization's objectives.[7]

It is easy to see how the domain of "strategy" has grown from the first definition to the last, as each has become more specific. The extent to which we should enlarge the term is important for our ensuing discussions.

Making the meaning of "strategy" too inclusive will only serve to make the term ambiguous, and destroy the reason for defining it. Yet the meaning of the term has been enlarged in recent years, mainly for three reasons.

First, the American business environment has grown more and more discontinuous because of the conditions of uncertainty under which it operates. Forecasting has grown more difficult, as is exemplified by erratic predictions of petroleum prices and interest rates. In order to function under such conditions of rapid change, company strategy must first be linked with current plans and near-term goals. Failures in this regard, growing increasingly common, are typified by the steel and automobile companies, and airlines.

Second, the rate of technological breakthroughs has greatly increased, as is demonstrated by the rapid proliferation of new products. This means that if American companies are to compete with their international counter-parts, their strategic planning must be carefully synchronized with a solid research and development program. The use of computer technology can greatly improve the linkage of strategic planning with short-term management, as is illustrated by STRATPORT[8] and ELECTRIC STRATEGY.[9]

Third, as a result of the development of techniques of short-term management, it is now possible to link planning with programming. As our experience grows, we can expect to be able to develop more effective frameworks and methods of placing different time dimensions in the proper perspectives, and for quantifying qualitative information.

RECOGNIZING CONSTRAINTS INTERNAL AND EXTERNAL

The previous section clarified the place of strategic planning in management, gave an overview of the growing scope of strategy, and briefly explored the reasons for this growth.

This section will explore one of the most important prerequisites for formalizing effective strategic planning: knowing oneself. Unless an organization knows its own strengths, weaknesses, and potentials, there is no way it can move forward. It is vital for an organization to be fully aware of its constraints, both internal and external, in order to understand its power fully.

External Constraints

External factors that affect a contingency framework are generally seen as political and military, technological, naturally caused, and economic. There are also less tangible external constraints, such as legal and social, that will not be discussed here.

Political and military factors can cause such basic changes that they require scrapping of the original strategic plans, and their reformulation from scratch. Recent examples are the cases of social unrest in South America and the Middle East that have led to the use of armed forces, with the result of scrapping international investment projects. Another example took place recently in the relations between Japan and Korea, where Japanese resentment over South Korea's treatment of an opposition politician could have resulted in the halting of trade amounting to more than $6 billion annually.

Clearly, technological transitional factors have had the greatest impact on American markets and companies. Twenty or even ten years ago, for example, no one would have imagined that small calculators would become so inexpensive, that minicomputers and microcomputers would become so widespread, and that even language translators, although still primitive, would be well within our reach. Over this period increasing numbers of high-technology products have been produced by, first, West Germany and Japan, then by Taiwan and Korea, and finally by less-developed countries. So long as the advanced countries maintain leadership in the development of these technology-oriented products, this trend presents no problem to strategic planning. If, however, they fail to do so, companies in the developed countries will have to revise their strategic planning in order to catch up.

Naturally caused factors also must be taken into consideration in strategic planning. A hurricane, typhoon, or earthquake can easily change the profit picture of a company. Until we can predict such natural disasters as the Los Angeles earthquake of 1971 and hurricane Agnes in 1972, or at least learn how to mitigate their effects, they must be considered in annual and strategic planning.

Economic and trading factors can also be very important. The recent erosion of the U.S. position as the economic giant of the free world is a striking example. While some argue that the rise in petroleum prices was the cause, it is hard to accept this rationale, since West Germany and Japan, even more dependent on oil imports, have strengthened their positions. They have improved their business-labor-government relationships and, as a result, their competitive positions, in spite of almost total dependence on oil imports.

Clearly, for American business to regain its competitive position, it will have to make larger investments in research and development, hold down wage increases, and improve productivity. Especially important is the development of a way to increase cooperation among business, labor, and government. Developing this cooperation is more important than any other challenge facing strategic planning in American companies today.

Internal Constraints

Internal constraints are those restrictions and limitations that occur within an organization. Bold and intelligent measures can frequently overcome them. Five representative internal constraints are the following:

1. Outdated management practices, due mainly to use of outdated management methods
2. Failure of research and development in a core product area
3. Repeated appearances of defective products
4. Bankruptcy of subsidiaries
5. Long-term strikes.

At this point, it is well to remember that continued intracompany confrontation among a group of executives can be as destructive as any disruption caused by external factors.

A common characteristic of internal constraints is that they are often not recognizable at once, and by the time they are recognized, they have already become serious. Recent examples are the Penn Central, Lockheed, and the Franklin National Bank crises. Particularly in highly decentralized companies, it may not be easy for the corporate or strategic planning office to find out what is going on internally, because decentralized units naturally try to hide weaknesses and exaggerate strengths. Three basic approaches may be used to overcome this trend toward distortion of information.

One is to create a centralized strategic planning staff—not simply a planning staff in each decentralized unit, but a staff through which linkage between headquarters and the decentralized units can be maintained. This linkage should not be limited to planning, but should also deal with budgeting and resource allocation.

The second approach is to have each decentralized unit reorganize itself into a strategic planning and control unit, as has been done to General Electric. The central objective in this approach is to control each strategic planning unit so that it reflects the corporate objectives and priorities. Each division must thoroughly understand the real intent of headquarters, and make sure that all its planning, organizing, and control activities carry out this intent. This problem will be discussed in more detail in subsequent chapters.

The third approach is redesigning and strengthening the internal auditing system. Particular attention should be given to the area of EDP auditing. The loss incurred through fraud in connection with computers and communications systems in U.S. firms far exceeds that incurred in nonsystems areas. More effective methods of and approaches to EDP auditing need to be explored by the internal unit on a continuing basis. The damage to small and medium-size firms is especially severe.

In one way or another, every organization identifies both external and internal constraints on its operations. At AMF, for example, one strategic planning unit listed as the three constraints considered most important for successful strategic planning: marketing development factors, competitive factors, and risk factors. Each of these is divided into four or five auxiliary factors.

General Electric at one point set up 42 strategic business units, mainly along product lines, each with contingency plans that identified their individual constraints. From these 42 units, 34 contingency plans were chosen as most important and were submitted to top management.

Hofer identifies 53 strategically significant environmental and organizational variables (see Table 1.1), but he goes on to show that, theoretically and practically, many of the variables are interrelated or have a negligible impact on the organization's overall performance.

Two questions naturally arise: In what manner should these variables or constraints be treated for further consideration? To what extent should we pursue each in order to ensure effective and successful strategic planning?

THE INEVITABLE NECESSITY OF STRATEGIC-PLANNING-ORIENTED BUDGETING

To understand the above, we must look again into the ultimate purpose of the corporation. There are three reasons why we must reexamine this much-discussed issue.

First, business, society, and government have grown increasingly interdependent, whether it be in the cooperative or the confrontational mode. International business activities and the growth of multinational corporations

TABLE 1.1. Strategically significant environmental and organizational variables.

Broader Environmental Variables	Industry Variables	Market, Organization and Consumer Variables
Economic conditions	Type of product	Market/consumer variables
GNP trend	Degree of product differentiation	State of the life cycle
Interest rates	Number of equal products	Market size
Money supply	Price/cost structure	Seasonality
Energy availability	Economies of scale	Cyclicality
	Degree of automation	Market segmentation
Demographic trends	Degree of integration	Buyer concentration
Growth rate of population	Experience curves	Buyer needs
Age distribution of population	Marginal plant size	Buyer loyalty
Regional shifts in population	Optimal plant size	Elasticity of demand
	Rate of product's technological	Purchase frequency
	change	
Sociocultural trends	Transportation and distribution	Organizational variables
Life-style changes	costs	Market share
Consumer activism	Barriers to entry	Degree of customer concentration
Career expectations	Critical mass for entry	Quality of products
		Value added
Political/legal factors	Competitor variables	Length of the production cycle
Antitrust regulations	Degree of seller concentration	Newness of plant and equipment
Environmental protection laws	Aggressiveness of competition	Labor intensity
	Degree of specialization in	Relative wage rate
Supplier variables	the industry	Marketing intensity
Degree of supplier concentration	Degree of capacity utilization	Discretionary cash flow/gross
Major changes in availability of		capital investment
raw materials		
Major changes in conditions		
of trade		

Source: Charles W. Hofer, "Toward a Contingency Theory of Business Strategy," *Academy of Management Journal* 18, no. 4 (1975): 798.

have accelerated the interdependence and broken through traditional national boundaries. In this process, corporations have shifted from domestic concerns to global concerns. Few executives today, regardles of the size of the company, can be concerned only with domestic profitability, welfare, and improvement. Today the objectives must include the welfare of the corporation as a whole, and of the international society it serves.

Second, the unanticipated speed of technological growth, especially in computers and communication, has enabled executives to accomplish things previously impossible. Lengthy, detailed computations and study of alternatives, previously impractical because of the time required, are now routinely undertaken and will continue to become even easier.

Third, a movement has arisen, usually expressed in the form of legal and legislative constraints, to ensure the welfare of, and provide better living standards for, people of all nations. These aims should be welcomed by corporations, and a government-corporation-workers coalition should be developed to see that they are implemented fairly, reasonably, and in a nonharmful manner.

These three developments have had a great effect on shaping the purposes of the modern corporation: to foster the welfare not just of the stockholders but of all people; to employ the most advanced technology in order to produce the best products or services possible; and to establish a stronger coalition with government and workers.

Clearly, if a company fails to experience satisfactory growth as a result of strategic planning, the welfare of even the local community cannot be improved. The stockholders' equity and the wealth of the company cannot be enhanced. And, to compound the problem, sluggish development creates pernicious long-term effects by causing the company to reduce its investment in the future (research and development), thereby weakening its competitive position. This is exactly the position of many U.S. and European companies today. Thus the basic question is simply "How does one reverse this situation so that the company's development is again on a healthy basis?" Strategic-planning-oriented budgetary planning and control is one of the most effective ways of "turning the company around." This requires the entire strategic planning process to be reevaluated through resource allocation. This requires us, first, to find the best possible strategic planning appropriate to each organization and, second, to find the best approach through which the strategic planning can be transformed into budgetary planning and control. The former is, in one sense, a reading and idea-conceiving process, while the latter looks for the advantages of one alternative over another in terms of comparative marginal return, present net value, or any other appropriate evaluation criterion.

More concretely, if computerizing an order-entry system is one strategic option in a small firm and an increased sales force is another, we will need to predetermine the return per unit dollar spent on the former compared with the latter, both independently and interdependently, to identify their priorities in our strategy.

Traditionally, this may not have been the job of the manager (in a small firm) or the corporate planner (in a larger firm), but may have been left to a budgetary specialist or a systems analyst. Now, however, with computers and telecommunications equipment we can inexpensively and quickly generate the relevant quantitative data.

Designing a monthly, weekly, or even daily budget is now possible, and companies adopting such budgets for marketing and production control are generally enjoying good growth. The time horizon of budgetary control is usually related to some other function, such as the life cycle of a product or seasonality. There is no reason now why budgets cannot be prepared on a time basis appropriate to the function controlled. This possibility, along with the uncertainty, discontinuity, and turbulence of our times, should make clear the necessity of strategic planning-oriented budgeting.

Strategic planning should not end with the recognition of problems and development of ideas, nor with resource allocation. It should also be used to assure and reassure the effectiveness of resource allocation on both long-term and short-term bases, in the presence of discontinuities. It should be the result of profound analysis and insights of top management, supported by carefully prepared computations. It should not be used merely to impress stockholders and outsiders. In all cases it must reflect the management philosophy and doctrines of the organization.

Strategic budgeting, therefore, is not just a process or procedure. It is the outcome of dedication to the solving of problems, taking into consideration all contingencies and productivity estimates.[10]

Strategic budgeting should be, on the one hand, an expression of the beliefs of the chief executive officer and, on the other hand, a product of in-depth computations that encompass all sorts of even remotely possible alternatives, in which a normative framework of a desirable future should be envisioned and progress toward it continuously evaluated. It should be a continuous process, not just a once-a-year task.

It is important to recognize that strategic budgeting is a thinking process about what and how to produce, and how to control future resources, regardless of environmental changes. It should help us overcome concerns about limited resources, inevitable total war, and doomsday. Above all, it should help us to pursue the happiness, peace, and justice that have so long eluded us, by identifying value-added resources and their most desirable allocation, and reallocations.

FRAMEWORK OF THE BOOK AND KEY TERMS

This book has been written for use by management and budget practitioners. They may be executives in smaller firms, who may require strategic budgeting more than ever; managers in medium or large companies; or controllers, accountants, and other specialists in firms of every size.

It should be noted that the necessity has arisen more than ever for owners, executives, and managers of small firms to introduce and implement strategic budgeting. Despite the fact that 97 percent of all businesses are small, that small firms employ 57 percent of the work force, and that small businesses generate 45 percent of the gross national product and have created nearly 70 percent of the new jobs in the United States since 1975, in 1980 approximately 10,000 small businesses failed, leaving behind $4.64 billion in liabilities.[11]

In order to meet their specific needs, considerations, illustrations, and cases involving small firms will be given wherever the author feels necessary. This of course does not mean that the book is meant for managers and specialists in the private sector only—the concepts and applications of strategic budgeting will be equally valuable for administrators, planners, accountants, and all others involved in budgeting, in industry, nonprofit organizations, health care and educational institutions, religious organizations and foundations, government, associations, societies, and related institutions.

Teachers and students of planning and budgeting will also find this book of interest and value, particularly for the many suggestions on how to organize and implement strategic planning and budgeting. The term "planning," used repeatedly throughout the book, must be distinguished from "forecasting" or "predicting." Planning is a process by which future action is determined; forecasting and prediction are the outcomes of analyses, and are not held responsible for future actions. We establish planning on the basis of forecasting or predictions. Forecasting is a rough picture of the future with which we are concerned. It should be greatly processed and refined before it becomes planning, which is realistic and meets the objectives of the corporation.

Planning must also be distinguished from budgeting. Although interactions between planning and budgeting are inevitable, in the author's view, budgeting is basically established on the basis of planning. Budgeting is the form of planning upon which resource allocation is established. Budgeting can also be called a quantified plan, since it cannot be complete without some form of financial statement with additional quantification, such as the number of people or units, the amount of energy needed, and so on.

Two representative types of planning, among the many, are long-term and short-term. Planning for three to five years or more is commonly considered long-term; for a year, short-term. Two- to three-year planning is sometimes called intermediate, or medium-term, planning.

Long-term planning has been replaced rather recently by strategic planning, and short-term planning has been referred to as operational planning. These terms are business-function-oriented rather than time-oriented. When the term "strategic planning" is used, the planning is related to top-management planning on a long-term basis. It should be related, therefore, to formulating and revising corporate missions and objectives involved in acquiring, employing, and dispensing tangible and intangible resources, such as material, human, and financial resources and information.

In the author's view, the essential differences between long-term planning and strategic planning are summarized as follows:

First, long-term planning is not greatly concerned with introducing a new product into the market to establish a firm hold on the market or to enlarge market share, or with withdrawing from a market; these considerations should be carefully considered in strategic planning.

Second, while competitive advantage is not seriously considered in long-term planning, it is a must in strategic planning. Since there are competitors and hostile environments to contend with, we must establish strategic planning to enable us to win over the competition, or to avoid unnecessary competition without incurring penalties.

Third, while long-term planning has tended to be based on past performance, strategic planning is aimed at creating the future position of the corporation, utilizing judgment, research, and in-depth computations reinforced by firm convictions.

There are three intrinsic differences between strategic planning and operational planning. First, strategic planning is more inclusive and integrative; operational planning is associated with a specific operation or task.

Second, while strategic planning is the process of foreseeing and setting objectives, operational planning is the process of determining whether a particular operation is to be undertaken. Therefore, evaluation of operational planning can be carried out in a short time, whereas the evaluation of strategic planning requires a much longer period.

Third, strategic planning is done by top management, on a much longer time basis, while operational planning is carried out by middle or lower management, with a shorter time, usually one year or less.

Where the term "management" or "managerial planning" is used, it refers mainly to middle management, which determines the effective acquisition, employment, or disposal of resources established by top management. In terms of the time horizon, management planning falls between strategic planning and operational planning—that is, about three years.

The term "strategic planning and budgeting," or simply "strategic budgeting," defines an integrative endeavor of strategic planning and budgeting control. It should reflect management philosophy and company doctrine. It is not simply a process or procedure, but is the outcome of analysis of all possible production, environmental, and competitive factors involved.

In addition to the nature and necessity of strategic budgeting, the historical background, management procedures, representative techniques, transition and implementation, case studies, and the future direction of strategic budgeting will be discussed in the ensuing chapters.

NOTES

1. Ram Charan and R. Edward Freeman, "Planning for the Business Environment of the 1980's." *The Journal of Business Strategy* 1 (Fall 1980): 11.

2. .Joel E. Ross and Michael J. Kami, *Corporate Management in Crisis: Why the Mighty Fall* (Englewood Cliffs, N.J.: Prentice-Hall, 1973), p. 21.

3. Ibid., p. 22.

4. Ibid.

5. C. Roland Learned. C. H. Christensen, Kenneth R. Andrews, and Joseph L. Bower, *Business Policy—Text and Cases* (Homewood, Ill.: Richard D. Irwin, 1973), p. 107.

6. Robert N. Anthony, *Planning and Control Systems: A Framework for Analysis* (Cambridge, Mass.: Harvard University Press, 1965), pp. 16, 17, 18.

7. Richard F. Vancil, "Strategy Formulation in Complex Organizations," *Sloan Management Review* 17, 2 (Winter 1976): 4.

8. An abbreviation of STRATegic PORTfolio Planning, a decision support system developed to aid managers in the evaluation and formulation of business portfolio strategies.

9. A new generation of electric utility models developed by MVN Micro Models with microcomputers.

10. American workers in many cases have had no better incentives than those of Japanese and West German workers, so that worker initiatives in productivity may be rewarded with both cash and praise. See, for example, L. C. Thurow, "Productivity: Japan Has a Better Way," *New York Times,* February 8, 1981, sec. 3, p. 2: 6.

11. According to a survey on the use of strategic budgeting approaches in small manufacturing firms, 52 percent of the firms prepared a set of short-term objectives, but very few of them put the objectives into writing. The owner or president was personally responsible for the entire objective-setting process in 22 percent of the 32 firms having short-range objectives. It was found that 11 of the 62 firms (18 percent) had written long-range plans. Only 14 of the firms prepared monthly budgets. For more detail, see Charles R. Stoner, "Planning in Small Manufacturing Firms: A Survey," *Journal of Small Business Management* 21, 1 (Jan. 1983): 34–41.

Linking of Strategic Planning
with Budgeting
—2—

In this chapter we will first establish a broad overview of the relationship between planning and budgeting, from the viewpoint of budgeting. Second, we will focus on a particular aspect of planning, strategic planning and budgetary control. Finally, we will discover a methodology by means of which we can design and develop successful strategic budgeting, and study some illusrations of it.

SERIOUS PROBLEMS THAT ARE FACED

One of the most serious problems faced is the complete independence of the planning function in relation to the budgeting function. There were several reasons for this. First, as business organizations grow, there is a widespread tendency to go from a centralized organization to a decentralized one. This has worked to develop more specific or specialized functions, including the planning function.

The planning function has evolved from very short-range planning to annual planning, from annual planning to long-range planning, and from long-range planning to strategic planning. In extreme cases planning is considered to be an envisioning process, and therefore independent from budgeting.

From the 1950s through the 1970s, such functions as production planning, market planning, financial planning, and corporate planning proliferated, and influenced the development of organizations. In general, planners benefited from opportunities for promotion to better positions, both within and outside the company, than the accountants who took care of the budgeting.

Separation of these functions may be feasible when a company is young and growing rapidly, with unsophisticated planning and an uncomplicated budget. However, the "good old days" do not last forever, and companies functioning in this way are soon faced with serious growth and profitability problems.

Second, the planning consumes a lot of time. Nevertheless, planning never provides an absolutely correct answer. Even though reading the future is in essence impossible, planners must undertake to do so, and there are always uncontrolled factors that may affect the course of operations in the future. Recognizing all the relevant factors in advance is almost impossible. The more time planners devote to planning, the less likely they are to look into other functions. For the amount of work put into planning, the results are not always sufficient. If unforeseen factors cause things to get worse, the planners are generally held accountable. This means, of course, that they will concentrate on planning, often to the exclusion of other important functions.

Third, planning demands inspiration, shrewd intuition, foresight, and something like a sixth sense. All of these, supported by an educated guess, may still not be sufficient.

The human characteristics needed for planning are often quite different from those needed for budgeting, though the former may be useful in establishing a budget. Budgeting, particularly in the traditional sense, requires a clear and logical mind, steady concentration, accuracy in calculations, and candor.

REMEDIAL ACTIONS TAKEN

Obviously, the separation of planning from budgeting can do nothing to facilitate the planning and control function, and must eventually interfere with normal, sound business activites.

In order to remedy the situation, we tried, first of all, to stop thinking of planning and budgeting as separate functions. Doing this greatly increases the chances of synchronizing planning with controlling—that is, budgetary control. Conceptually, this was accomplished at first by means of capital budgeting, and later by project or program budgeting.

In addition, the organizational framework has such sections or departments as planning and budgeting, or profit planning and control. These sections or departments normally deal with planning and budgeting functions in an integrative manner. Even if gaps develop in the earlier stages of planning, they can be quickly adjusted by frequent interaction between the planning and budgeting specialists.

As program budgeting is shifted to PPBS (Planning, Programming, and Budgeting Systems) or to zero-based budgeting, the general trend toward integration of planning and budgeting is greatly strengthened.

RELATIONSHIPS BETWEEN VARIOUS BUDGETS AND PLANS

As shown in Table 2.1, using the "2 x 2" matrix produces four elements by which we can show the integrated products developed from both budget and plan.

It is quite common to divide budgets into incremental (traditional) and comprehensive (modern) types, whereas plans are classified as short-range or long-range. As a result we will have at least four different budgets, using those plan and budget types.

For example, a sales-oriented budget based on cash flow and budgeting via a standard cost system illustrates a short-range plan and an incremental budget. This

TABLE 2.1.   The relationships between types of budgets and plans.

Type of Budget	Programming Tactical plan Short-range plan	Planning Strategic plan Long-range plan
Traditional budget Incremental budget Static budget	Sales-oriented budget based on cash flows	Capital budget Research and development budget
	Operational budget with standard cost systems	
Modern budget Nonincremental budget Comprehensive budget	Zero-based budget Priority-oriented budget	PPBS (Planning, Programming, and Budgeting System) Program budget

Source: Prepared by author.

is one of the typical budget systems being adopted by many private companies as well as by organizations in the public sector. In the latter, sales would be replaced by services rendered.

At the right of the table are illustrations based on incremental budgeting and a long-range plan, such as capital budgeting and research and development budgeting.

Incremental budgeting is a method in which only an increment is of major concern. We are talking about how much we have to increase the budgets in terms of dollars or percentages, without looking into the entire accumulated body of the budget. While this method saves time and concentrates on one of the very important aspects—the increment—it does exclude an analysis of the entire budget, as accumulated up to the previous period, for the purpose of removing or updating the obsolete portions.

Since the incremental budget has no possibility of a decrement, a significant problem lies within the budget itself. (More detailed discussion of this is in Chapter 3.)

Zero-based budgeting or priority-oriented budgeting is an outcome of comprehensive budgeting and a short-range plan, while PPBS is considered to be the result of a long-range plan and comprehensive budgeting. The latter is often called a program budget when it is established on the basis of the programs that are the more specific portions of planning. Since a program is defined as the smallest unit of planning, it is often called a planning unit.

For example, an overall missile development program is a plan, while MX missile development may be a planning unit in the area of national defense or international security. For another example, a personnel development program is a plan, whereas an executive development program is a planning unit.

Zero-based budgeting incorporates discontinuous thinking or planning. Its basic concept is to think from zero. This type of budgeting is in sharp contrast with incremental budgeting, in that no budget increase is warranted unless it has fully feasible reasons to support it.

The important advantages of zero-based budgeting are that it offers the possibility of reducing the budget, which is not easily done in traditional budgeting, and that it is possible to incorporate a priority plan into the budgetary process (hence priority budgeting). An additional advantage is the opportunity for consideration and incorporation of opportunity costing, wherein an assumption is made that the cost is eliminated. If the results of eliminating the costs are too dangerous, we will be forced to include the cost in the budget. If not, we can eliminate it.

Although we will discuss this in Chapter 3, we should now have an understanding of the representative budgets and the plans with which they are generally used. Among the short-range, incremental budgets are operational budgets, including sales, cost of goods sold, inventory, purchasing, gross margin, expense, and (eventually) net income. Pro-forma income statements, balance sheets, statements of earnings, and cash-flow statements are also considered in short-range, incremental, and zero-based budgets.

An ABC budget is a derivation of the zero-based budget in which a priority scheme is simplified and normally categorized into three classes, such as optimistic, most likely, and pessimistic, or most necessary, necessary, less necessary.

For example, in Yonkers, New York, the A budget contains more than is presently planned; the B budget matches the present budget, with adjustment for inflation; and the C budget is a contingency budget including only the minimum levels of services and expenditures. "Minimum level" is the lowest level of activities that will still allow one level of the budgetary units to survive. (A more detailed explanation is in Chapter 3.)

At S. A. Schonbrunn and Company in New Jersey, A, B, and C budgets are differentiated as follows:

A budget, a budgetary project that should be accomplished by all means

B budget, a budgetary project through which incremental benefits are to be obtained

C budget, a budgetary project that involves great risk but also offers the possibility of great returns.

At Parsons and Whittemore:

A budget, the most important budget

B budget, also an important budget, but can be omitted if necessary

C budget, a desirable budget, although, if savings are more important, it can be omitted.

As can be seen from the above, A, B, and C budgets are classified in terms of necessity and urgency.

Allocation is a derivative of zero-based budgeting in which allocations are not only financial but also related to human, information, and other intangible requirements. This is another area where, because of the growth away from traditional, limited allocations to indirect cost areas, zero-based budgeting should be further extended. A, B, C, and allocation budgets are regarded as either short- or long-range comprehensive budgets, generally less comprehensive than the original version of the zero-based budget. Inasmuch as the budgeting process is time-consuming, it is desirable to investigate the possibilities of computerization. If we have reached the stage at which we can separate repetitive and nonrepetitive processes, computerization becomes easier.

STRATEGIC PLANNING AND BUDGETING

Now that we have had an overview of the relationships between types of plans and the forms of budgets, we will narrow the relationships between strategic planning, one form of long-range planning, and comprehensive budgeting.

In fact, as shown in Table 2.1, the terms "long-range planning" and "strategic planning," an outgrowth of the former, are both used. Strategic planning that is an action plan of corporate strategy should be based directly on corporate objectives and goals. The more accurate and achievable the corporate goals are, in the light of present capabilities, the greater the likelihood that an effective strategic plan will be formulated. A business circle of the 1980s, as shown in Figure 2.1, should place primary emphasis on the adequate formulation of strategic planning, to be followed by strategic programming that should include both new strategic units and existing strategic units that can be easily shifted into preparation of the strategic budget.

Once the strategic budget has been established, it is carried out after going through various forms of review and approval. The results will be evaluated by means of performance measurement criteria, and a performance report will be issued to facilitate implementation and enhancement of the strategic budget as well as the strategic planning.

In the next section, we will examine strategic planning in more detail: first, as processes and procedures; second, how it is intertwined with the budget and interacts with it; third, means of implementing the relationship between strategic planning and budgeting.

FIGURE 2.1.   The relationship between strategic planning and budgeting.

STRATEGIC PLANNING AS AN ACTION PLAN

Strategic planning should be an action plan through which a company can improve its position, both internally and externally. External improvement should involve foreign as well as domestic improvements.

In order to accomplish this, both general and specific strategic plans must be established. The former should include environmental predictions, with contingencies, opportunities, and threats in the light of the strengths and weaknesses of the corporation, and the position of the product line.

The ultimate objective of the overall plan is to determine what should be accomplished, on the basis of what is possible. Differences between what is desired and what is possible can often be resolved by introduction of new products, revision of the product mix, change of processes and procedures, intensification of research and development, or mergers and acquisitions.

A specific strategic plan may also be called a strategic project. It should contain development programs for new products, all the important research and development programs, all the programs designed to build up sales, all programs for major investments in buildings and equipment, all programs related to increasing efficiency (including productivity, improvement of learning and experience curves, and incentives), and all programs relating to design and development of information and computer systems.

This plan should, directly or indirectly, reflect programs related to product lines, the divisional operations program, corporate programs (usually in the form of pro-forma financial statements), and additional reports, including remaining unresolved issues and supplementary plans for emergencies.

An Overall Strategic Plan

This plan should start with a very careful review of the past, and piercing insights into the future. The period must include at least the past ten and next ten years, in order to identify the crucial factors that did affect, and might in the future affect, the existence of the company. Accordingly, it is very important to reexamine the entire history of the company, and its distant future, with special attention to the ten most important variables or factors that have had, and could have in the future, tremendous impact on the company. They may be environmental factors, such as depressions or earthquakes, or internal ones related to the failure of a reorganization or of research and development.

After identifying these factors, we move to the environmental prediction, including the general trend of politicoeconomic and socioeconomic factors, technological factors, and specific quantitative information, such as gross national product, personal consumption expenditures, and personal income.

For example, along with the divorce rate, the birth rate to unwed women may be important; births to unwed women increased noticeably in the 1970s, and now at least one of every six American babies is born to an unmarried mother. This will have an effect on the babies, who will be more mother-centered. If these women play the father's role in the traditional sense, the unisex trend will be promoted, which will affect consumer behavior.

A general trend search may be required to determine the expectations of all types of people: managers, employees, stockholders, creditors, clients, government officials, lawyers, other professionals, and the general public. This will indicate the nature of the society that will evolve in spite of hurdles set up to prevent change.

If peoples' expectations are too high to be fulfilled in the present society, they must be persuaded to lower those expectations. If they still cling to them, a different socioeconomic order becomes a necessity. If a new order is not created as required, the society is moving into jeopardy. Research may need to determine the societal needs for future years, and to find out whether they will be met.

For example, when a union is trying to win wage increases to meet expectations of the employees, but demand and productivity are low, can the company (and, on the larger scale, corporate society or the nation) satisfy their demands? Obviously not.[1] If the company grants the wage increase, its deficits will mount to the point where it must seek financial aid from the government. In turn, the government's deficit will reach the $1 trillion mark sooner.

We must visualize the outcome of this untenable situation of the 1980s and determine what radical changes will be required to rectify the situation.

It is self-evident that in a free-enterprise system, products must become cheaper and better. If they do not, there is no way they can compete. If major products are not competitive in the open market, it is useless to waste time on marketing or strategic planning for them.

Strategic planning is meaningful only when the products involved are competitive (or will be competitive at a certain point). If they are not, the government should take steps to assure that the products remain competitive. Few consumers will be happy buying cheaper, better foreign products while they are unemployed.

For these reasons, future market analyses should include as part of the environmental prediction conclusions based on future competitive capabilities in relation to major foreign companies as well as domestic firms. We must be thoroughly familiar with the quality and price of our competitors' products as well as the marketing strategy they plan to deploy against us in the 1980s.

In an overall strategic plan, the next step after the environmental prediction is the analysis of opportunities and threats. "Opportunities" means positive aspects that offer the chance to build up programs, while "threats" means negative aspects that affect our strategic planning. The former include the opportunity to develop foreign operations and sales, new products, a new enterprise, and a desirable merger or acquisition. Threats include saturation of demand, obsolescence of a product now in the growth stage, more severe competition, restrictive legislation, shortages of raw material, and political unrest.

Clearly, the objective of strategic planning is to weaken or evade threats, and to take maximum advantage of opportunities. When analyzing threats and opportunities, the scenarios established are usually in terms of optimistic, most likely, and pessimistic. Both assumptions and results should be supported by some sort of quantitative analysis.

The third step, after the analysis of opportunities and threats, is the analysis of performance, strengths, and weaknesses of our own organization. First of all, performance should be reviewed and summarized in the light of, for example, fundamental goals, strategic thrusts, internal structure and characteristics, and productivity. Second, the strengths and weaknesses should be analyzed in terms of performance against competitors on major performance indices such as sales, return on investment (ROI), earnings per share (EPS), and debt-equity ratio; the present states of strategic planning areas, such as top management, business development, corporate planning, and laboratory; marketing strategy; competitiveness of each product; and the products' advantageous characteristics, such as faster sales, higher profitability, cost, and technological attractiveness.

The fourth, but not least important, step is an appraisal of our own products. This can be done by either product portfolio management (PPM) or portfolio impact of marketing strategy (PIMS) and equivalent techniques.[2] If we decide to use them, we will need a worksheet to use in determining the place of our products in comparison with major competitors or in the market as a whole.

Once the place is determined, we have to come up with an overall strategy. It may be determined in advance, or as a result of accumulating specific approaches for each product line. Since each product line cannot be totally independent of the others, it is often sound policy to design an interaction matrix for each product, in order to identify efficiency and structural problems that might decrease synergistic effects.

At this stage, the differences between what we can do and what we should do are clarified to a great extent, and we are ready to construct an overall strategy.

Specific Strategic Plan

This plan can first be established by each division or group by product lines, and then by headquarters on the basis of an overall strategic plan, or it can be used in the construction of the overall strategic plan. The details of each specific plan are normally attached.

A specific strategic plan should encompass both a comparatively wider-scope project and the specific project. The former may entail the transformation of the composite of product lines, new product development, strengthening of the sales force, overseas advancement projects, rationalization of production and ordering systems, reorganization, and personnel projects. The latter should be specific enough to state the project concretely, on a time-series basis.

For example, for a new office automation project, a new company will be established at the end of 19__ in cooperation with company X and company Y. This company will be 50 percent owned through Offauto, one of our subsidiaries, with company X and company Y owning 25 percent each. Initial capital of the new company will be $5 million, (Financial and personnel strategies follow.)

Another example is building a new Institute of Bioengineering by initially spending $10 million, with the objective of becoming a leader in the field in five years. (Areas of study, personnel, yearly programs, and goals will follow.)

New-product development projects must be in harmony with the product life-cycle strategies already established. If a newer and better product appears in the market sooner than expected, we must accelerate our own product development. This may, in turn, require advancing the implementation of yearly, personnel, and other programs. The new products development project should also be synchronized with the changes in the product life assessment, and with the movement of the location of our products on the PIMS or PPM matrix.

Attention must also be given to the establishment of the products withdrawal program and the new products introduction program. If the introduction of new products gets behind schedule, every effort should be made to prolong the life cycle of the established product so that a smooth transition may be made. However, planning should be perceptive enough to realize that the introduction of a new product may not mean the start of its growth. Some new products may have a longer embryonic period.

The essential differences between an overall strategic plan and a specific strategic plan reside in demographic, geographic, and timing specifications, and with production and marketing segmentations. However, the essential idea is that both must be mutually supplementary. If overall strategic planning cannot cover certain aspects, such as local market uniqueness or the extraordinary attractiveness of one product, those aspects should be fully covered in specific strategic planning.

Equally, very important factors and elements of the specific strategic planning should be noted in the overall strategic planning, and in its implementation and enhancement, by being included in brief form. What is really important is that the specific strategic planning does not eliminate specific factors that influence overall strategic planning. On the other hand, an overall strategic plan should not omit any contingencies or other factors difficult to foresee.

INTERACTION OF STRATEGIC PLANNING WITH BUDGETING

Bearing the objectives, scope, contents, process, and procedure of strategic planning in mind, let us further explore the place where strategic planning and budgeting interact.

First of all, in the overall strategic plan all the quantitative indirectly, related to budgeting, particularly sales, and direct labor and material costs. If we are in a consumer industry, the projection of real personal consumption expenditures over the next ten years must be directly related to sales. The availability of raw materials is another variable that will affect costs.

Therefore, it will be helpful to distinguish between the information directly usable to evolve sales or cost-of-goods-sold budgets and information not usable for the immediate needs. Certainly, economic factors are among the many factors that influence both sales and cost-of-goods-sold budgets. Internal factors, such as marketing, distribution, advertising, and research and development costs should also be developed by our planning efforts. To project future demand effectively, using both internal and external factors, we will have to construct some sort of a demand projection model.

This is particularly important because one of the external factors, competition with foreign companies, is one of the most important areas and demands constant updating. It is very difficult to design and develop demand projection models, using available quantitative information, unless we fully understand the behavioral patterns and individual strategies of the competition. Most of the failures of U.S. companies stem from lack of understanding of these factors.

Therefore, the initial interaction point between strategic planning and budgeting should be considered very seriously. Some more detailed suggestions will be given in the next section.

In addition to these readily available tangible factors, the intangibles, such as demands of future stockholders, changes in rules and regulations, and even possible settlements of lawsuits, must be taken into consideration. These can be summarized in the expectancy impact shown in Table 2.2. Quantitative transformation is always possible by scoring each expectancy.

While the analysis of opportunities and threats helps in the development and implementation of demand and cost modules, the analysis of our own performance—strengths and weaknesses—will have much greater impact on the various aspects of any kind of budget.

For example, if we look at the table of analysis for our own performance, we note that in addition to sales and cost-of-goods-sold budgets, income, advertising promotion, R&D, and distribution budgets are also interrelated, as shown in Figure 2.2.

The more we analyze the strengths and weaknesses of our own company, the more closely the various budgets will be interrelated. By linking these budgets with the total budget, we will be in a good position to review the feasibility and effectiveness of our strategic planning from the viewpoint of vital resource allocation.

In specific strategic planning, we arrive at the stage of more detailed linkage between strategic planning and budgeting. Each strategic project is related to an independent budget, which may be a capital budget, a research and development budget, or any other budget or combination of budgets. It is of course most desirable to incorporate these specific budgets into the overall budget in an orderly manner.

An "overall budget" is an integrated budget incorporating all the specific budget components, including project budgets, less important strategic project budgets, and common strategic project budgets. Common strategic project budgets include all budgets with factors in common, such as headquarters and logistics-related budgets.

As will be explored in Chapter 4, each strategic budget, common or specific, will be formulated by means of a package that includes objectives, scope, description

TABLE 2.2. Expectancy impact.

Personnel Concerned	Total Number	Direction of Expectations			Relative Importance for Survival	Relative Importance for Growth	Extent of Dissatisfaction
		Now	*+1*	*+5*			
Executives	12				extremely important	very important	very high
Managers							
Employees							
Union members							
Stockholders							
Creditors							
Clients							
Suppliers							
Communities							
Public							
Government— federal and local							
Foreign							

Note: A detailed description of each should be attached. A scoring system can be incorporated, such as 5 = extremely important; 4 = very important; 3 = important; 2 = less important; 1 = not important.

Source: Prepared by author.

of inputs and outputs, expected findings, assessment of cross-impact, impact of eliminating the strategic project concerned, performance measurement, and evaluation criteria.

Each package will be prioritized through review, and should be designed so that it can be implemented when necessary. The position and significance of each strategic package can be continually evaluated, so as to avoid weakening the overall strategic position.

This process is very similar to zero-based budgeting, although the contents of the package are different. They are longer-term-oriented, cross-impacts are more fully explored, and multiple projections are made in the light of discontinuity, uncertainty, and turbulence.

HOW TO STRENGTHEN THE RELATIONSHIP BETWEEN STRATEGIC PLANNING AND BUDGETING

In order to synchronize strategic planning and budgeting, we make both institutional and procedural changes. The former are to establish a new department or section called planning and control, or planning and budgeting, while the latter are to design and develop new budgets, such as program budgets or zero-based budgets.

Therefore, in order to strengthen the linkage of both, we must adopt effective approaches. This means that if institutional strategic planning and budgeting are independently located or prepared, reorganization should take place at the earliest possible opportunity.

If both departments have already started to integrate the processes, the initiative should be taken by the department whose efforts are further along and the integration should be incorporated into the reorganizational plan.

In addition to the reorganization and establishment of the new department or section, the content of budgeting should be revised to incorporate the nature and substance of strategic planning more effectively.

Effectiveness can be a meaure of the value of strategic planning. The criterion for evaluation should be one that measures the value of the planning against the cost. The net value of the planning can also be measured against other approaches and actions through which the company might obtain superior results that were not known at the time the original strategic plan was prepared. Another measure of effectiveness of strategic planning is its ability to react to contingencies.

Efficiency is also a measure of the process of strategic planning. Processes and procedures that are too time-consuming and complicated reduce the efficiency of strategic planning. However, if the planning is simple and concise, but nevertheless contains all the substance, we can say that our strategic planning is efficient. Efficiency also includes timeliness and smooth flow between strategic planning and budgeting.

FIGURE 2.2.   Relationship among table of analysis of our performance, strengths, and weaknesses, and various budgets.

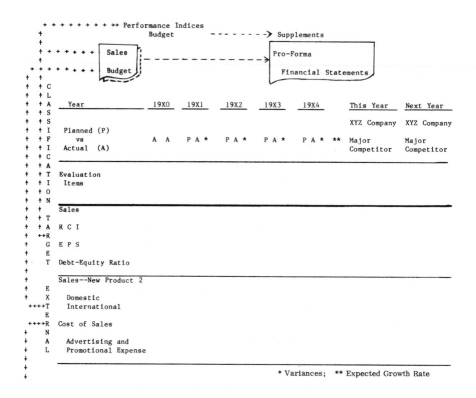

One of the approaches recommended in this book is strategic budgeting. As briefly touched upon in the previous section, strategic budgeting is an extension of zero-based budgeting. Its objective is to make the budgeting more easily applicable to both present and future environments.

Note, however, that this is not totally new. The evolution of budgeting has been long, and in general, development has been continuous as zero-based budgeting has corrected the weaknesses of program budgeting and PPBS. In one sense, it can also be said that the present era of governmental and private budgeting called for zero-based budgeting to justify needed budget reductions.

Strategic budgeting, as the name implies, must facilitate strategic planning and management. In this sense, a strategic budget is more specific than a general budget. Strictly speaking, strategic planning should precede strategic budgeting, so

FIGURE 2.2. *(continued).*

Year	19X0	19X1	19X2	19X3	19X4	This Year	Next Year
						XYZ Company	XYZ Company
Planned (P) vs Actual (A)	A A	P A *	P A *	P A *	P A * **	Major Competitor	Major Competitor

Evaluation Items

Direct Labor
Direct Material
Overhead
Inventory
R&D

Sales Costs

Budgeted Direct Labor
Budgeted Direct Material
Budgeted Overhead
Expense Budget
Operational Budget (19X2)
3-Year Operational Budget
R&D Budget

that the details of the budget can be developed without the stresses of urgency and contingency. A strong inclination toward merger or acquisition by our company may require a discontinuous transformation of an established budget on the basis of competing with the other companies.

Also, strategic budgeting is by nature comparative budgeting, in which the competitor's strategic planning and budget cannot be neglected. Such information is the basis on which more effective analysis and implementation of strategic planning can be founded.

Although it is extremely difficult to continually trace the competitors' strategic planning and budget, hiring a person who has worked in the specific area of the competitor, hiring a consultant who is familiar with the competitor's strategic planning and budget, and establishing a specific data base in this area, so that updated information may be continually gathered through external sources (such as newspapers, trade journals, and reports), are some of the measures to consider.

Finally, strategic budgeting is by nature multiple long-term budgeting—that is, it is designed to be effective under conditions of uncertainty, discontinuity, and turbulence. Such conditions reinforce the need for credible information. The lower the credibility, the more likely it becomes that the quantity of information available will decrease.

Of course, strategic budgeting is not the sole method of strengthening the linkage between strategic planning and budgeting. Many other behavioral and technological methods can enhance the relationship. The development of information systems with an emphasis on global or semiglobal intelligence and information bases utilizing extremely large data bases, the evolution of telecommunication technologies, and computerized budgetary planning and control models will certainly facilitate closer relationships beween strategic planning and budgeting.

When the planning-equals-budgeting era arrives, our planning will become explicit and succinct; and cooperation with other companies, both domestic and foreign, in an intelligent manner will be possible. For instance, in the Fifth Generation of Computer Project in Japan, representatives of competing firms are beginning to work together.

In the final section of this chapter, an illustration will be provided to clarify the discussions and procedures related to strategic budgeting compared with traditional budgeting.

CASE STUDY

Let us assume a case where ABC International (ABCI) has established a beautiful overview, as shown in Figure 2.3, and where Mr. Spearhead, director of strategic budgeting, asked John First, a planning analyst, to elaborate each phase of the strategic planning system. Spearhead also said that, as a result of the elaboration, he expects to have a variety of means through which strategic planning and budgeting may be effectively linked. At Stage 1, however, John had to devote his time to strategic plannning, bearing in mind the establishment of appropriate linkages with budget.

When John was given the assignment, he first took a close look at the strategic planning system. He noticed that there were three components in strategic planning, and that two were linked to strategic programs. Access to budgeting can be gained directly from the strategic programs.

FIGURE 2.3. An overview of a strategic planning system.

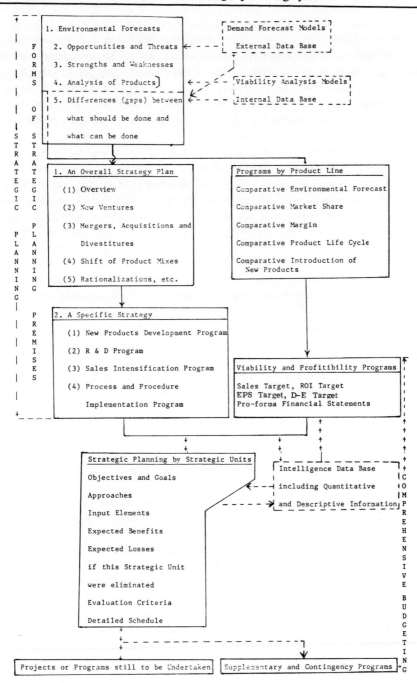

Being aware that the aim of the premises phase is identifying the differences between what should be done and what can be done, he decided to work first with the form of environmental forecast. However, he felt that "prediction" would be a better word than "forecast," since judgment processes might need to be incorporated.

After studying the possible judgment factors (which may include normative factors), John decided to include a table of key issues to help prevent him from overlooking major environmental factors. This form is shown in Table 2.3. He felt very strongly that this table should be implemented as the process proceeds. After constructing the table and developing enough responses, he turned to the production of a table of environmental forecast.

John felt that this table should contain a general overview as well as a specific forecast of environmental variables. For the former, he decided to include a societal trend, with emphasis on the policy established by the office of the president and the predispositions of his advisers; a legislative trend, with emphasis on relevant laws and regulations; an economic trend, in terms of inflation and recession; a financial trend, including interest and prime rates; a technological trend, with emphasis on the discoveries and inventions of major competitors; and an international trend, with emphasis on the development of overseas markets and political factors. There were many other important factors, but John reasoned that an overview should not be too long, and trends that were not really important should not be included.

When investigating the forecast of specific variables, John checked the company's available models as well as the variables discussed by users of the strategic planning system. He isolated 15 variables as most important and related to variable budgets in some manner, and decided to include additional specific forecasts in the appendixes. The form is shown in Table 2.4

John next turned his attention to a table of opportunities and threats analysis. He studied the records of the executive committee, or the strategic planning and control committee, to determine the exact meaning of opportunities and threats in ABC International. In addition, he reviewed the strategic planning and budgeting records in order to summarize the opportunities and threats. The result was Table 2.5.

Since he felt that the shift of opportunities into threats should be recorded in a systematic manner, John decided to include a PIMS matrix and a threat-influence matrix, to indicate how to evade or cope with the possible threats, as appendices. He also set up scenarios for dealing with threats and opportunities.

John's next task was a table of analysis of major products. It seemed too complex to summarize everything in one table, so he determined the most important variables and criteria. Consequently he designed one and put the less important data in separate charts to be appended. Among the factors included were a detailed analysis of the company's own products, their position in the market and relevant strategy, in-depth evaluation of the product mix, and identification of the products to be introduced and withdrawn.

TABLE 2.3. A table of key issues.

Key Areas	Key Issues
Corporate policy	What sort of business should we engage in?
	What sort of customers should we seek?
	What sort of major products should we manufacture?
	What sort of major services should we render?
	What sort of image should we establish?
	What sort of basic attitude should we establish?
Social responsibility	What preventive and follow-up actions should we take on ecological matters?
	What contributions should we make to the community?
	What actions should we take to reduce the accident rate?
	What actions should we take to improve product quality?
Growth and profitability	What sales figures should we maintain?
	What should be our return on investment?
	What should be our earnings per share?
	What should be our debt/equity ratio?
	What should be our sales/total cost ratio?
	What should be our average growth rate over the next five years?

31

TABLE 2.3. *(continued).*

Technological breakthroughs	What technical leadership should we achieve?
	What research and development effort should we make?
	What innovations should we make in the areas of production, materials, labor, advertising, and promotion?
Market strategy	What place should we establish in our industry?
	What place should the present product maintain?
	What place should the new product achieve?
	What place should the present product maintain in a new market?
	Where should we develop a new product?
Financial strategy	What should be our total capital?
	What financial mix should we maintain?
	What is the best way to keep our financial structure healthy?
	What relationships should we establish with securities and financial markets?

Material resources	How large should the scale of facilities and equipment be?
	What reliability and maintenance requirements should our machinery and equipment have?
	What should be the operating rate of our machinery and equipment?
	What sort of facilities should we keep?
Human resources	What sort of executives and managers should we have?
	What sort of capabilities must our employees have?
	What moralaity should we foster?
	What salary, wage base, and incentives should we establish?
	What relationship should we establish with the union?

TABLE 2.3. *(continued).*

Productivity	What should be an appropriate level of productivity?
	What should be adequate for productivity on capital (added value)?
	What should be adequate productivity for services?
	What should be adequate productivity for administrative services?
Overseas strategy	What should be the size of our overseas markets?
	What product mix should we maintain for present overseas markets?
	What distribution channels should we use to increase sales in overseas markets?
	What clients should we seek in overseas markets?

Source: Prepared by author.

34

By doing this, John felt he could identify the crucial differences between what his firm should do and what it could do. Particularly, he felt he should set up items that would highlight comparative advantages and disadvantages of each major product. The outcome is shown in Table 2.6.

Although he used both differences and ratios to highlight the advantages and disadvantages of the company's products and lines, John felt that this was still not enough. He felt that any particular advantages and disadvantages should be noted, and a detailed analysis appended.

In addition, the crucial objectives of the comparative studies should identify the individual competitors, analyze the present characteristics and the potential of the competition, and provide effective action to compete with them successfully. "Competitors" includes both present and future competitors, and John realized that an extremely important function of strategic planning is to identify competitors that are not obvious now.

In order to find potential competitors as soon as possible, John realized that he had to follow up on their research activities, explore the quality of their research personnel, and determine the effectiveness of their information systems, both domestic and international.

Consequently, he added a table on the competitors' activities, information development (including the sources of their information), available hardware, software, and human resources.

As a result, John was convinced that in order to clarify the difference between what ABCI should do and what ABCI can do, he must first identify the key issues that are the foundation of the next task, an environmental assessment and prediction. On completing this, he must analyze opportunities and threats so that the actions that can be taken are clear. Then he must link this analysis with an analysis of ABCI's products and product lines compared with the industry as a whole and with major competitors to find out what should be accomplished. Finally, differences between what can be done and what should be done will be clarified. Although there are many other factors to be taken into consideration, John believed that this approach, supported by these materials, would function as a basis for any further development.

The next job for John was to design the form for an overall strategic plan. He felt that since differences between what should be done and what can be done will be described in a variety of terms, such as institutional (new ventures, mergers and acquisitions), functional (changes of product mix, building of quality-control circles), and financial (sales increase, ROI, and/or EPS), the form should be able to accommodate these terms, as well as additional items he could not think of at the moment. As a result, he designed a rather flexible form for an overall strategic plan.

Still another task was the preparation of two forms in terms of product lines: one a specific strategic plan and the other a strategic program. He thought that

TABLE 2.4. Environmental predictions.

Overview of environments

Societal trend
Political trend
Legislative trend
Economic trend
Financial trend
Technological trend
International trend

Specific forecast

Items	Unit	Rate of Increase (decrease)	Actual	Estimated	+1	+2	+3	+4	+5	Rate of Increase (decrease)
							Year			
GNP										
Optimistic										
Pessimistic										
Corporate profits										
Real individual consumption expenditures										
Per capita income										
Consumer Price Index										

36

Wholesale Price Index

Exchange rate

Unemployment rate

Interest rate

Prime rate

Gross private investment

State of labor force

Labor turnover

Hourly earnings

Productivity indices

Source: Prepared by author.

TABLE 2.5. Opportunities and threats analysis.

	Year						Notes*
	0	+1	+2	+3	+4	+5	
Opportunities							
Increasing sales of product A							Adequate
Possibility of overseas markets							Replacement
Introduction of product X							4
Introduction of product Y							5
Possibility of a new business line due to R&D							
Possibility of acquisition of Company E							
Possibility of joint ventures with Companies F and G							

Threats

Decreasing sales of product B   2

Ceasing domestic competition with
  Companies H and I

Increasing legislation   7

Possible shortage of materials J and K

Possible price increase of raw
  material L

Impact of new technologies on
  products and production methods

Political and social unrest in country M

Scenarios

Optimistic
Most likely
Pessimistic

---

* The numbers are page numbers of supplementary materials or appendices.
Source: Prepared by author.

TABLE 2.6. Analysis of major product lines.

Major Items	Product Line X	Product Line Y	Product Line Z
Relevant industry			
Industry sales			
Industry growth			
Forecast—next five years			
Retrospect—last five years			
Average ROI			
Average EPS			
Average debt/equity ratio			
Major competitor			
Annual sales			
Growth			
Forecast—next five years			
Retrospect—last five years			
Annual ROI			
Annual EPS			
Debt/equity ratio			

40

Our company	Self	Competitor	Self/Competitor	Self	Competitor	Self/Competitor	Self	Competitor	Self/Competitor
Annual sales									
Growth									
Forecast—next five years									
Retrospect—last five years									
Average ROI									
Increasing (decreasing) rate of ROI									
EPS average									
Increasing (decreasing) rate of EPS									
Average D/E ratio									
Sales/cost ratio									
Market share									
Market share ratio									
(own market share/ competitor market share)									
R&D costs									
Sales/ R&D ratio									

Note: "Self" denotes own company; "Competitor" denotes major competitor. "Self/Competitor" denotes the competitive ratio between self and major competitor.

Source: Prepared by author.

TABLE 2.7. Strategic plan, by project and strategic unit.

PROJECT PRIORITY / COMPONENT	1. Total Costs directly con-tributable to projects or programs in a SU		2. Total Costs indirectly attributable to projects or programs in a SU		3. Total Earn-ings directly attributable to projects or programs in a SU		4. Human Resources, Incremental or Decre-mental in a SU		5. Increment of market size, market share in a SU		6. Incremental ROI and Residual Income in a SU	
	Actual	Est.	Actual	Est.	Actual	Est.	Actual	Est.	Actual	Est.	Actual	Est.
	+1+2+3+4+5		+1+2+3+4+5		+1+2+3+4+5		+1+2+3+4+5		+1+2+3+4+5		+1+2+3+4+5	

Notes: Project Priority:
A — Very Important
B — Important
C — Less Important

A: Actual

E: Estimated

SU: Strategic Unit

42

these plans should be project-oriented, and that time-series data would be required. He realized that these forms, too, should be strategic-project- or strategic-program-oriented so that each could be easily linked with the strategic package.

He decided to include the project name, its priority, a description of the project including objectives and goals, total direct costs, investment costs, total benefits, incremental and decremental human resources, incremental or decremental market size and share, incremental or decremental ROI, and residual income. The result is shown in Table 2.7.

Although unsure of what information should be included in the form of strategic budgeting, the best component John could think of was some sort of strategic package that explains the strategic program or project in detail. In this case, he reasoned that the substance of a specific strategic plan should be the integrative form for strategic budgeting.

Fortunately, John had studied PPBS and program budgeting, and worked for a company using them. It seemed to him that this concept and approach would be the best for his company. To confirm his thinking, he discussed his idea with Mr. Last, who had had experience with zero-based budgeting. Mr. Last told John that his idea was a good one, and suggested that John study the project further, so that the forms he proposed could be used to contribute the maximum to the development of the company.

NOTES

1. To survive under these conditions, one possibility might be to establish an employee stock ownership trust. See the case of the Hyatt Bearing plan of GM Corporation. *New York Times*, October 26, 1981, sec. 4, p. 1:3.

2. These techniques were originated and developed by the Harvard Business School and General Electric along with several consulting firms: Reston Consulting Group, Arthur D. Little, Mackinsey, and Strategic Planning Institute.

Comparison of Traditional and Strategic Budgeting

—— 3 ——

In this chapter we intend to compare traditional budgeting and strategic budgeting, particularly in regard to typical issues encountered in traditional budgeting. Then we will highlight the place and significance of strategic planning in a total business cycle of organizational planning and control.

COMPARISON OF TRADITIONAL BUDGETING, ZERO-BASED BUDGETING, AND STRATEGIC BUDGETING

As summarized in Table 3.1, the comparison can highlight the evolution of budgeting systems.

First of all, the philosophy may be described most simply as moving from function to program and from program to strategy, following traditional, zero-based, or strategic budgeting procedures. This transition from process to procedure is best represented by movement from accounting to decision making and from decision making to implementation. These changes have been made necessary by the change from justification for the increase of old programs to justification for both old and new programs, and from that base to the justification of old, new, and unique programs.

Second, from the viewpoint of technique or method, traditional budgeting adopted extrapolation, assuming that past trends would continue, usually with a periodic increase and adjustment for inflation, while zero-based budgeting adopted a quite different approach. It breaks up the budget into the smallest independent budgeting units possible, called decision packages, analyzes and ranks them, then adopts all the decision packages above the cutoff line, in descending order.

Strategic budgeting is intended in principle to use the same approach taken by zero-based budgeting. However, the nature and characteristics of strategic packages are different from those of decision packages, in that strategic packages are more long-term-oriented; they deal with uncertain and discontinuous factors that require more multiple estimates to be included; and they should incorporate the results of cross-impact analyses to a greater extent.

44

TABLE 3.1. Comparison of traditional, zero-based, and strategic budgeting.

Attributes	Traditional Budgeting	Zero-Based Budgeting	Strategic Budgeting
1. Philosophy	• Function-oriented (by division and department)	• Program-oriented (e.g., production or service)	• Strategy-oriented (by position, strengths, and weaknesses)
	• Accounting-oriented (primary focus on "how much?")	• Decision-oriented (focus on "what," "why," and "how" issues as well as "how much")	• Implementation-oriented (focus on "what" first, and then "how" as well as "how much")
	• Focused on justifying new incremental programs	• Requires all programs, old or new, to compete for the same scarce resources	• Requires extensive new and unique programs
2. Techniques	• Extrapolate past spending	• Break up budget into independent decision packages	• Break up budget into independent strategic packages
	• Increment for inflation and new programs	• Analyze all packages and rank them	• Analyze all strategic packages, including cross-sectional analysis, and rank them
	• Trim, usually across the board, to achieve affordable level	• Trim only discrete, marginal programs and packages up to the level of affordability	• Establish a flexible cutoff line, depending on an allowable budget

45

TABLE 3.1. *(continued).*

Attributes	Traditional Budgeting	Zero-Based Budgeting	Strategic Budgeting
3. Linkages to long-range plan	No linkage to long-range plan exists. If claimed, it is lip service at best. If budget indicates that plan is unachievable, attempts to reconcile the two are rarely made	Requires integrated linkages from budget side to strategic planning. By constant reiteration of the process, both plan and budget are brought into agreement	Requires integrated linkages from strategic planning side. Budgetary control further facilitates the linkages. By constant, effective use of the method, both plan and budget are coordinated
4. End product	An aggregated set of numbers, often bloated beyond affordability and understood by few, if any. Long hours usually spent in bringing preliminary submissions to reasonable levels	A clean, lean, muscular set of ranked priorities that can be increased, changed, or trimmed as circumstances warrant, in a rational manner	A clean, lean, muscular set of ranked priorities, with uncertainties that can be rationally increased, changed, or trimmed, as circumstances warrant
5.a. Organizational impact with staff	Encourages "gamesmanship." Those who substantially inflate requests, knowing they will be cut, are implicitly rewarded by winding up with what they probably wanted. At the same time, those with responsible submissions are penalized by the inevitable cuts. Few make the same mistake twice	Facilitates rational analysis and decisionmaking: Those who do inflate their packages are more likely to be caught and exposed. Carefully devised, results-oriented packages make heroes of their sponsors.	Facilitates more integrated analysis and key decisionmaking. Those who inflate their decision packages are more likely to be screened and requested to justify the package. Insightful packages will contribute to the objectives and goals of the organization

46

5.b. Organizational impact between staff and budgeting	The situation is polarized. Time is "dummy-up" time. Communications often break down. As a result, plans made by the staff are likely to have nothing to do with budgeting efforts. Overlapping plans and misallocation of limited resources will ensue	All options are laid out for open discussion, mutual evaluation, and agreement in a businesslike atmosphere. Triggers need for and use of selling skills within and between staffs to persuade each other of merits of their proposals and to manage the changes required by approved programs	All allowable options are laid out for open discussion, mutual evaluation, and agreement in a businesslike atmosphere. All possible triggers, including selling skills and piercing insights, are used within and between staffs, to persuade each other of merits of their projects and to manage changes required by approved programs
5.c. Organizational impact between staff and top management	The burden of proof is placed on top management to decide how much should be spent for what, and why	The burden is placed on staff members to show why they should spend anything at all—with top management making final decisions on an orderly, rational base of ranked priorities	(same as at left)

TABLE 3.1. *(continued).*

Attributes	*Traditional Budgeting*	*Zero-Based Budgeting*	*Strategic Budgeting*
6. Personnel impacts	Known to lead to high turnover and morale problems, not to mention divorces and ulcers	The system is clean, responsible, and responsive. Where cuts are needed, feedback can be more convincing and tactful because cuts are put into the context of the organization's broader objectives, needs, and resource limitations	The system is clean, responsible, adaptive, and comparative. Where cuts are needed, feedforward and feedback can be more convincing and tactful because the cuts are put in the context of the organization's philosophy, goals, objectives, needs, and resource limitations
7. Preventive controls	Difficult to achieve in a timely manner because system is essentially backward-looking	Easy to initiate in a timely manner because system is comparatively forward-looking	Very easy to initiate in a timely manner because the system is very forward-looking

8. Follow-up controls	Relatively easy to translate into follow-up control mechanism. However, the spending being controlled may not represent the best use of the organization's resources	With appropriate procedures and forms, decision package can be readily rolled up for a conventional follow-up control system. More important, specific major results-oriented problems can be monitored to make sure they achieve the crucial objectives and not just a targeted spending level	With appropriate procedures and forms, strategic packages can be readily rolled up for a modern preventive control system as well as a conventional follow-up control system. Specific major results-oriented programs can be monitored to make sure they achieve the crucial objectives and not just a budgeted spending level
9. Participatory characteristics	Normally limited to executives, managers, and budget specialists who are directly involved in budgeting, planning, and control	Not limited to executives, managers, and budget specialists, but includes any employees who are concerned with better resource allocation for the future. Participatory in nature	Participatory in nature. However, more effective participation is expected, particularly from executives and managers, for achieving feedforward control
10. Linkage to other business systems	Gradual linkage is being established by those companies that still use traditional budgeting and traditional, line-by-line-oriented budgets	Basis for organizational planning; could logically be linked to a manpower planning and use system that facilitates movement and develops key performers	Business systems so duplicative or redundant that efforts can be minimized; linkage with external and large-scale data base systems will be inevitable

Third, in traditional budgeting, linkage to a long-range plan, usually received only lip service and no satisfactory linkage was established. Zero-based budgeting, on the other hand, aims for linkages between the budgeting side and long-range planning. If linkage is to be developed, constant attention is required to coordinate planning and budgeting. Strategic budgeting, as the name implies, places the major emphasis on linking strategic planning with budgeting from the planning side; strategic planning is considered to be a revised form of long-range planning.

Fourth, from the viewpoint of controls, it is difficult to take preventive control action in a timely manner with traditional budgeting. In zero-based budgeting, it is easier because it is forward-looking. More specifically, controlling difficulties in advance is one of the primary reasons for establishing and implementing zero-based budgeting. This concern is of even greater importance in strategic budgeting because without successful strategic planning, budgeting is useless, no matter how well the limited resources are allocated and reallocated.

In regard to follow-up controls, even if traditional budgeting has an effective follow-up control mechanism, that does not guarantee the best use of the organization's resources as far as the limited scope of the objectives is concerned. In zero-based budgeting, decision packages, which are reviewed on a broader objective basis, make effective vehicles for containing the follow-up mechanism. The broader review helps to assure the effective allocation of organizational resources. Strategic budgeting stresses this aspect even more: the use of limited resources for broader, more quality-oriented objectives.

Fifth, while in traditional budgeting, participation is generally limited to executives, managers, and budgetary specialists, in zero-based budgeting it is not limited to those; any employee who is concerned with developing more effective resources and evaluation can work on it. Zero-based budgeting therefore may be viewed as participatory budgeting. In strategic budgeting, while participatory budgeting is incorporated, participation by executives and managers concerned with strategic planning is required. Budgetary procedures can always be established on the basis of effective planning.

Finally, in regard to linkages with other business systems, all budgeting systems, except for very traditional ones, have been paying attention to this factor. However, much greater attention is paid to linkages in zero-based budgeting than in conventional budgeting. Since zero-based budgeting is designed to allow easy detection of duplication through linkage with other business systems, such as marketing, personnel, and R&D, a more rational basis may be instituted for organizational planning than is possible with traditional budgeting. Strategic budgeting also takes careful account of the linkages with other business systems. The basic difference between zero-based budgeting and strategic budgeting on this point is that in strategic budgeting, the major emphasis is placed on the linkage with strategic planning systems, while zero-based budgeting systems tend to give equal emphasis to linkages with all other business systems. In strategic budgeting, linkages with environmental information systems and large data-base systems should be given careful consideration.

This difference results from the natures of the two systems; although there is a general trend toward long-term orientation, zero-based budgeting systems are operational in nature, and strategic budgeting is strategic in nature, as the name implies. Therefore, any subsystems in the zero-based budgeting configuration that are inadequate should be carefully revised and strengthened.

In summary, the differences between zero-based budgeting and strategic budgeting rest on their central emphasis: newness versus uniqueness, linkages with the strategic versus dynamic long-range plans; decision packages versus strategic packages; rational analysis versus integrative analysis; and operational versus strategic natures.

In the next section, we deal with the typical issues brought forth in zero-based budgeting, and discuss how to solve them by means of strategic budgeting in order to implement state-of-the-art budgetary planning and control.

TYPICAL ISSUES RAISED BY ZERO-BASED BUDGETING

While zero-based budgeting is the most up-to-date and effective system, and has achieved the greatest impact in both private and public areas since PPBS, it is not perfect or without deficiencies.

As pointed out by Minmier[1] and others who evaluated or were involved in the design and development of zero-based budgeting systems, one of the most serious deficiencies is the time and effort required to prepare the budget. Some organizations felt that the benefits of zero-based budgeting were not worth the time and effort, and discontinued it; others continued using it because they felt that both tangible and intangible benefits exceeded the cost of the time and effort required.

Still another group of organizations was seeking more appropriate approaches that would be more acceptable. Their actions may be summarized as follows:

1. Avoiding repetition of the same item from the beginning every year, once zero-based budgeting was instituted
2. Recognizing that variety in introduction and implementation exists
3. Evolving smoothly and steadily, without haste (for example, one transition would be from the incremental, line-for-line-oriented budget to the zero-based budget via the program budget).[2]

Another deficiency concerns a psychological factor: the frustration and resistance to change resulting from the possibility of being laid off as a result of changes in policies, procedures, and systems, as well as of reduction of personnel costs arising from the change.

These psychological issues have surfaced whenever a new concept or technique is introduced, and in most cases they have been resolved by leadership of top management; an official announcement that there would be no layoffs, even if underutilized personnel were discovered; and written clarification of the objectives and policy issues in a new planning and budgeting system.

The third deficiency has to do with the design, organization and evaluation of a decision unit and a decision package.

The deficiencies mentioned have been corrected or will be corrected as more experience is accumulated. The U.S. government and many private corporations, such as New York Telephone, Mead, Xerox, and Parsons and Whittemore have revised their manuals for annual zero-based budgeting to make the definitions and instructions on the decisions unit and decision package more concise, and have added more pertinent illustrations, so that various approaches and methods that are suitable to each organization can be found and implemented.[3]

It should be pointed out, however, that although zero-based budgeting has been in use for several years by both private companies and government agencies, two issues are still unresolved: the ranking and the selection of the level of efforts.

The fundamental issue involved in ranking is this: to what extent can we be objective and justify our ranking, so that the essentially subjective ranking process will make possible the objective fulfillment and accomplishment of the program? Ranking methods include individual and group methods (such as conference, voting, and conference-voting methods), single-stage and multistage ranking methods, closed ranking (ranking done by persons inside the organization), and open ranking (ranking done by persons both inside and outside the organization). It is certainly desirable for each organization to select the method best fitted to the planning and budgeting process.

In general:

1. As to ranking within a decentralized division (or department) with similar functions, at the initial (or an early) stage of ranking, closed ranking is desirable. If necessary, a decision package may be integrated or removed. Even integrated ranking (to reorganize two or more decision packages into one solid package, and then ranking) can be done
2. As to ranking between or among two or more different functions, a ranking or evaluation committee consisting of the personnel in each key function must play an active role in ranking each decision package on an overall basis.

Last, with respect to selecting a level of efforts, there seem to be three basic questions: how to decide the minimum level of efforts; how many levels of efforts need to be established once the minimum level has been set up; and how many alternative packages should be designed.

Although 80 percent has been rather widely adopted as the minimum level of efforts it should be noted that this number must not be rigidly adhered to or standardized before exploring to find the minimum appropriate to each organization.

The numbers applied to the second and third deficiencies have ranged between two and ten. There is no legitimate reason, however, why the number of levels or alternative packages must fall into this range. As computer-based zero-based planning and budgeting (ZBPB) becomes more and more common, and as our creativity develops, enabling us to increase the number of decision packages, it will also be possible to generate more sophisticated levels of effort along with the increased number of packages.

Following are some of the considerations that may form the basis for choosing an appropriate decision package.

CONSIDERATIONS IN SELECTING AN APPROPRIATE DECISION PACKAGE

First, don't establish a level of effort that does not meet intrinsic objectives. In Table 3.2, we cannot select any of the decision packages designed. The packages that should be selected are not what kind of telephone systems to produce, but in what manner marketing is to be executed: television, magazines, newspapers. (Producing a particular telephone system has already been decided.)

Second, don't set up a minimum level of effort that is higher than the predetermined minimum level. As shown in Table 3.3, when the requirements set up by the Federal Communications Commission are met by establishing a minimum level of 70 percent of last year's budget for the analysis of depreciation expenses, there is no need to set up a higher minimum level, say, 85 percent, to meet the requirements of the Public Service Commission.

Some of the important factors to be considered as the basis of the minimum level of effort are whether it is lower than the present level of efforts; whether discretionary cost consideration is included; and whether it will sustain the core of the present program.

Third, achieve a balance between the increment of required expenses and the alternatives. There have been cases in which the size of the increment of required expense is not uniform for all the objectives of decision packages. This indicates that the analysis of the objectives of a decision package has not been made fully.

For example, in Table 3.4, the increment from 3 of 4 to 4 of 4 is excessively large and the objective itself is too inclusive and ambiguous. Therefore, it should be

TABLE 3.2. Decision packages and objectives.

Decision Package	Objective (Description)
4 of 8	Produce convertible (indirect) communication system
5 of 8	Produce a direct communication system for managers
6 of 8	Produce automated response and recordable communication system

Source: Prepared by author.

TABLE 3.3. Percentages of budget versus objectives.

Compared with Last Year's Budget	Objective (Description)
70 percent	To study the minimum depreciation expenses requested by the FCC
85 percent	To complete the study on the analysis of depreciation expenses requested by the PSC

Note: The minimum level of 70 percent is not changed unless a lower level is requred.
Source: Prepared by author.

TABLE 3.4. Required expense versus objectives.

Level of Effort	Required Expense	Objective
1 of 4	69.8	Respond to the basic cost analysis
2 of 4	52.2	Complete both required and subsidiary assignments
3 of 4	23.7	Make voluntary cost analysis of a specific job
4 of 4	170.3	Make cost analyses for all jobs supporting corporate planning

Source: Prepared by author.

divided into three to five smaller objectives. Examination from a different angle may reveal that 1 of 4 through 3 of 4 can be consolidated into a single package.

Fourth, don't include unrealistic requests or assumptions to be applied unilaterally to other divisions or departments. For example, when a pensions department sets the implementation of a life insurance claims procedure as one of the objectives of a decision package, but plans to leave the matter to each regional center, where there is no capability to deal with the claims, this decision package should not be accepted.

Another case would occur when an education department establishes a decision package whose objective is to develop a computerized order/entry system, the responsibility for which would be left to the personnel department, which has no capacity to handle such a system.

A further example would be to expect those who earn MBAs to educate the company employees regarding a newly purchased telecommunications system. Because a majority of them will leave the company when their education is completed, such an objective in the decision package is meaningless.

In these instances, it is vital to identify the capabilities of each decision unit to which duties and responsibilities might be assigned. If the needed capabilities do not exist, it must be decided in advance what remedial action, with appropriate budgeting, will be established.

Fifth, describe adequately the objectives (contents) of each decision package in the light of each level of effort. Errors are most frequently due to too broad or too narrow descriptions. For example, in one company "95 percent of the managerial training requirements must be met" was one of the objectives of the decision package. However, the requirements were unclear and many interpretations of the word "requirements" were possible. On the other hand, there are cases in which the descriptions are so detailed that they look as if the budgeting decisions had already been made.

STRATEGIC BUDGETING AS AN EXTENSION OF ZBPB

The author identifies four major ways to improve and implement ZBPB: more long-term (or strategic planning)-oriented budgets,[4] more extensive introduction of rational and behavioral methods, computerization, and integration.

More Long-Term Oriented Budgeting

It is accepted that ZBPB is a planning and budgeting system for use in both the private and public sectors when a short-term (annual) budgeting system is to be established.

Consequently, although the linkage of ZBPB with strategic planning is well established, the outcome in most cases is annual budgeting figures. Certainly in the case of capital budgeting, where the effect of the budgeting over many years must be anticipated, annual figures are inadequate. There is no question that strategic planning should be fully integrated with both internal and external quantitative information.

In order to meet this need, a several-year budget, preferably three or more years, has to be designed and developed. This trend is expected to grow among private companies, regardless of size and experience level.

Among companies in which a partial adoption of ZBPB has been made, such as Westinghouse, AT&T, and Fujitsu, the application of ZBPB to capital investment decisions is not unusual. In this case, a long-term viewpoint is inevitable; therefore ZBPB would become even more completely integrated if strategic planning is used. In addition, the application of zero-based analysis will spread not only to administrative and staff areas, but to operational areas as well.

One budget year should reflect one cycle of program planning, organization, and control. Some organizations may require three years to complete a cycle, while others may need only three months. Although it will be seriously affected by external reporting requirements, more pressure toward longer budgeting periods will result from the present decline in American business, blamed by many on the shortsighted pursuit of immediate profits instead of the more important goals of long-term growth and profitability.

More Extensive Introduction of Rational and Behavioral Methods

Since ZBPB aims at solving issues by means of scientific approaches, especially management accounting and the principles of management, more extensive efforts will be required to introduce scientific methods (including both rational and behavioral methods in broader terms) to enhance the quality of information, rationalization and reallocation of resources, and implementation of decisions.

Especially from the aspect of management information, the methods and techniques developed in the area of information science (or, in a broader sense, software sciences) need to be applied. In like manner, issues in optimizing and the reallocating of resources require the application of mathematical programming and related techniques, and those in decision making need the techniques of decision sciences. All these methods and techniques must be integrated into the process of designing and evaluating decision packages and ranking tables.

In addition, we will need to develop cross-impact analyses, Delphi methods, and opportunity-cost analyses for foreign-exchange management[5] as methods of assessing interdependent effects, or as preliminary means of analyzing decision packages.

It will be easier to apply the above methods as the computerization of ZBPB advances. This will bring about the speed in evaluation and revision needed to increase the overall efficiency and effectiveness of zero-based systems.

Computerization

Computerized ZBPB systems have been designed and developed in the public and private sectors. The merits of computerization include saving time in repetitive operations, reduction of computation time in sophisticated calculations, increased efficiency in information retrieval, and more in-depth evaluation of alternative packages.

Computerized systems should certainly help increase the speed of implementation, which in turn should provide more quality-oriented information. There can be no doubt that computerization is an essential change if the state of the art of ZBPB systems is to advance. As more and more on-line interactive ZBPB systems are developed, administrators and executives will be forced to spend more time identifying feasible priorities in the light of corporate objectives, and establishing the comparative importance of the various decision packages.

From many recent interviews with executives of both public and private organizations that have introduced ZBPB, it appears that the problems of procedural details and repetitive work have been overcome by applying zero-based analysis only partially, or not at all, from the beginning of each year, but every two or three years, and by increasing computerization.

Computerization can be further utilized in the process of integration, discussed below.

Integration

It is the author's view that ZBPB systems will continue to grow, either by themselves, with ensuing development and integration, or as one of the most important subsystems of management information systems.

The growth can also be envisioned as shown in Figure 3.1, which depicts four major subsystems to be integrated—financial management, accounting control, personnel management, and work measurement systems—as well as presently available planning, programming, and budgeting systems (PPBS), management-by-objective systems, and resource allocation systems.

These subsystems will be integrated as a rational data base or in some other appropriate arrangement, so that budgeting, periodic review, and updating and implementation of data bases can be undertaken in a convenient manner.

The extent to which this implementation will be effective depends on the development of the concepts and techniques of ZBPB, on the one hand, and those of computer systems, on the other.

It is fully foreseeable that more effective, interactive models that reveal interdependent and value judgment issues will be employed in the future. This will be facilitated by the use of various types of computers, including mini-computers and microcomputers. Strategic planning systems will be more rigorously explored, with the intent of determining more feasible resource allocation in the light of both corporate and national growth.

FIGURE 3.1.   An integrated strategic planning and budgeting system showing direction of implementation and enhancement.

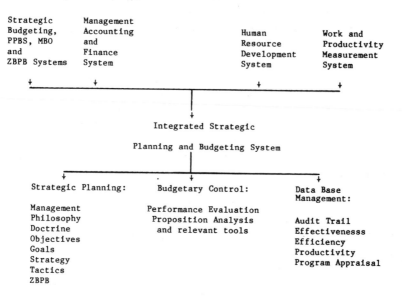

CONCLUDING REMARKS

We may visualize the development of ZBPB in the United States as more long-term (strategic planning)-oriented budgets, more extensive introduction of rational and behavioral methods, computerization, and integration. This view is based on the results of questionnaires, interviews, and the historical background of budgetary planning. It is clear that the major outcome of the extension of zero-based budgeting will be strategic budgeting.

Budgeting has always evolved through the interactions of the environment, the organization, and people. A common factor in the evolution and development of budgeting is the attempt to create a better future through procedural implementation, participation, and control.

The problems involved in creating a better future are more complex than in any previous period because of the shortages of resources, unbalanced allocation and reallocation of resources, and increasing competition and conflict in the military and trade spheres.

Although strategic planning is by no means a panacea, there is an intrinsic necessity to allocate misallocated limited resources in order to utilize them to the fullest extent. Thus, strategic budgeting should become one of the most important concepts and techniques to be developed in the years to come.

NOTES

1. See George Samuel Minmier, *An Evaluation of the Zero-Base Budgeting System in Government Institutions,* Research Monograph no. 68 (Atlanta: School of Business Administration, Georgia State University, 1975), pp. 168–69. Minmier states that there are two significant failures associated with the employment of zero-based budgeting in the state of Georgia: the inability of the new budgeting system to significantly affect the efficient allocation of the state's financial resources; and the ineffectiveness of ranking the decision package in meeting changes at the level of financing, in addition to the increased time and effort devoted to budget preparation.

2. See *Zero-Base Planning and Budgeting Digest* 5, no. 5 (May 1981): 2–5. The rest of this section is adapted from Akira Ishikawa, "A New Trend and Issues of Zero-Base Budgeting," *Kigyokaikei* (Enterprise Accounting) 32, no. 3 (March 1980): 88–94.

3. During the Reagan administration, the ponderous zero-based budgeting has been virtually eliminated, particularly in the Department of Defense, while the requisition system is linked to PPBS in the planning phase—that is, there is heavier linkage to resource allocation. For more details, see Jack R. Borsting, "Decision-Making at the Top," *Management Science,* April 1982, pp. 241–351.

4. For another treatise on this subject, see Akira Ishikawa, "Strategic Approach to Zero-Base Budgeting," in A. Ghosal, ed., *SCIMA Special Studies on Planning* (New Delhi: South Asian Publishers, 1980), pp. 141–151.

5. See for details, *The Proceedings of International Symposium on Zero-Base Planning and Budgeting,* Tokyo, National Institute for Research Advancement and Japan Productivity Center, 1974, pp. 57–93.

Management Procedures
of Strategic Budgeting
——4——

Since we have already considered the evolution of budgeting, the differences between zero-based budgeting and strategic budgeting, typical issues raised in zero-based budgeting, and strategic budgeting as the outcome of an extension of zero-based budgeting, it is now time to discuss the management procedures of strategic budgeting.

Once strategic planning is established, it should be transferred, in the form most suitable for linkage, into the resource allocation process. In Figure 2.3, this process is shown in terms of an overall strategic plan and a specific strategic plan (on the left-hand side), and of a viability and profitability program (on the right-hand side), as related to strategic planning by strategic units. Let us now look more closely at effective management procedures for transferring these plans and the program in such a way as to achieve the most successful resource allocation.

ESTABLISHMENT OF A STRATEGIC PLANNING UNIT

The basic question is: Once strategic planning has been established by a central strategic planning office, with full acceptance by top management, what organizational unit is to receive, interpret, and rearrange the planning into the form of resource allocation?

The answer should be a strategic planning unit, ordinarily established on the basis of product lines or business functions, because it is considered to be the smallest unit having an independent business mission, both conceptually and practically. This means the smallest unit to transmit strategic intent, and the smallest able to receive it and act on it. Each strategic planning unit should be a discrete entity with the following functions:

1. Plan, organize, and control independently
2. Identify distinct groups of customers and markets
3. Distinctively employ resources, technologies, and specialties
4. Face a distinct group of competitors
5. Possess its own capabilities to create and innovate.

In other words, the unit must be large enough to be viable and to grow under normal circumstances. Even in the worst case, each unit should have its own contingency plan. It should be noted that a strategic planning unit may operate on a single level or on multiple levels. In the extreme case of a small firm, a strategic planning unit may consist of one person, the owner of the firm.

If a strategic planning unit cannot meet all the requirements of strategic planning, then some other organizational unit should be so autonomous that it not only can satisfy those requirements but also, on its own, generate new strategies from which headquarters, or other strategic planning units, can benefit.

Now, to consider the function of strategic planning more specifically, let us assume that strategic planning unit A deals with the program for new product development (item (1), Specific Strategy, Figure 2.3). What sort of documents should the strategic planning unit prepare? In terms of flow of information, the analysis of products in the premises statement of strategic planning comes first. This is related to the shifts of product mixes in an overall strategic plan; as a result, the program for development of new products is created, along with programs for product lines.

As a result, Table 3.1 was prepared. Using this table, we can make further estimates of sales and cost of sales in order to determine acceptable gross margins, return on investment, earnings per share, and debt-to-equity ratio, based on pro-forma financial statements. These are, as shown in Figure 2.3, the programs on viability and profitability—that is, a preliminary analysis aimed at making a highly effective strategic (budgetary) package. We will go more deeply into the preliminary analysis in the next section.

PRELIMINARY ANALYSIS

One of the most important purposes of the preliminary analysis is to construct the most relevant (to strategic planning) and quality-oriented strategic packages for each strategic planning unit.

Therefore, various analyses should be performed in order to help crystallize all the requirements that are to be included in all the strategic packages. Typical methods of analysis include portfolio analyses, strategic financial and accounting analyses, and cross-impact analyses.[1]

While a product portfolio is denoted by four cells with two variables, market growth rate and comparative market share, more cells (ordinarily nine) are used in the PIMS model.

In addition, in PIMS two variables are selected (see Figure 4.1) to make cross-sectional or time-series analyses. The PIMS data base has shown that

FIGURE 4.1. PIMS matrix: comparative position of return on investment.

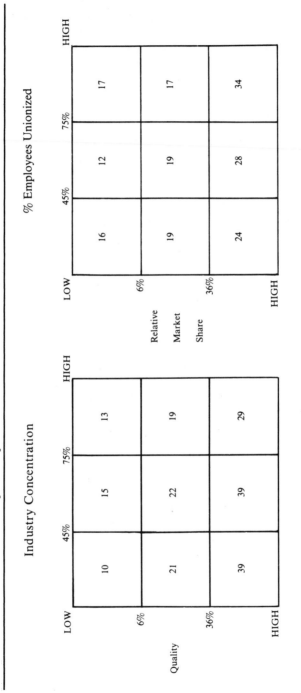

Note: Each number in the matrix denotes ROI. The left matrix shows that, in general, as both quality and industry concentration get higher, return on investment becomes higher. The right matrix reveals that, in general, while the increase of relative market share augments ROI, percent of employees unionized adversely affects ROI.

Source: Prepared by author.

about 30 factors describing a business and its competitive environment account for 70 percent to 80 percent of the observed variability of performance across diverse businesses.[2]

Whatever approach we use, the most serious concern should be how we can crystallize our products, or product lines, in a unique manner, in order to gain the maximum advantage over competitors. While these methods clarify our position and indicate what actions we should take, we must be aware that some of the major competitors may not take the same approaches, and thereby may not use the strategies we expect.

Even if the same approach is taken, we must discover some of the unique variables as well as the essential ones. For example, in PIMS the variables—such as the quality of products, value added per employee, and R&D productivity—may be considered unique. These may be defined in a number of ways that are quite different from the PIMS definition.

Comparative advantages should arise from the combination of these variables, as well as from each variable. If we establish a 5 percent annual growth in the next five years, the expected increment accruing to each of these key variables should be identified by a set of logicomathematical models. It may well be that the average increments of the quality of products and value added per employee in the next five years will equal 4 percent, while the average increment of R&D productivity might be 7 percent.

As more advantageous results arise from the increasing number of combinations of variables, our chances of succeeding in the ensuing competition increase. The sooner we can discover the weaknesses of our alternatives, the better we can prepare by thinking of a wide range of alternatives. The essence of preliminary analysis is to discover the feasibility and practicality of strategic planning, on the one hand, and to discover alternatives that will help us to attain objectives and goals, on the other.

Strategic financial and accounting analysis also is varied. What is common is the use of some sort of financial statement, either for external reporting or for internal control.

Let us assume that ABC International is preparing both a five-year pro-forma consolidated income statement and a balance sheet. These financial statements should satisfy the demands of objectives and various goals, such as growth, earnings per share, return on investment, labor and service productivity, cost control, and the others that are included in statements of strategic objectives and goals.

In the initial step, the work is equivalent to incorporating constraints into the financial statements. For example, if we take sales growth, the percentage of growth is specified over the next five years. Therefore, once the projected sales for the next year are determined, the succeeding four years can be determined automatically, as shown in Table 4.1.

TABLE 4.1. ABC International: Five-year performance statement of income and retained earnings, year ending Dec. 31.

19X3	Net Sales	Percent of 19X4	Net Sales	Percent of 19X5	Net Sales	Percent of 19X6	Net Sales	Percent of 19X7	Net Sales	Percent of
Net sales	$2,100	100	$2,940	100	$4,410	100	$7,056	100	$11,995	100
Operating expenses	1,993	94.9	2,760	93.9	4,097	92.9	6,484	91.9	10,903	90.9
Cost of sales	1,375	65.5	1,896	64.5	2,844	64.5	4,551	64.5	7,737	64.5
Selling, general, and Administrative expenses	618	29.4	864	29.4	1,253	28.4	1,933	27.4	3,166	26.4
Operating income	107	5.1	180	6.1	313	7.1	572	8.1	1,092	9.1
Nonoperating income/loss Nonoperating income	52	2.5	73.5	2.5	110	2.5	176	2.5	299.9	2.50
Interest dividends received	21	1.0	29.4	1.0	44.1	1.0	70.6	1.00	119.9	1.00
Other operating income	31	1.4	44.1	1.5	66.1	1.5	105.8	1.50	179.9	1.50
Nonoperating expenses	80	3.8	111.7	3.8	167.6	3.8	268.1	3.80	455.8	3.80
Interest paid	54	2.6	76.4	2.6	114.6	2.6	183.4	2.60	311.9	2.60
Other nonoperating expenses	26	1.2	35.3	1.2	53.0	1.2	84.7	1.20	143.9	1.20
Income before extraordinary items and income taxes	79	3.8	141.8	4.8	255.4	5.8	479.9	6.80	936.1	7.80

Extraordinary income	2.3	0.1	2.9	0.1	4.4	0.1	7.1	.0.1	12.0	0.1
Extraordinary loss	0.8	0.0	0.9	0.0	1.0	0.0	1.1	0.0	1.5	0.0
Income before income taxes	80.5	3.8	143.8	4.9	258.8	5.9	485.9	6.9	946.6	7.9
Income taxes	29	1.4	51.7	1.7	93.2	2.1	174.9	2.5	340.8	2.9
Net income	51.5	2.4	92.1	3.2	165.6	3.8	311.0	4.4	605.8	5.0
Retained earnings at beginning of period	15	0.7	20.6	0.7	30.9	0.7	49.4	0.7	83.9	0.7
Dividends paid	10	0.5	14.7	0.5	22.1	0.5	35.3	0.5	60.0	0.5
Provision for legal profit reserve	1	0.0	2.0	0.1	8.8	0.2	14.1	0.2	24.0	0.2
Retained earnings at end of period	55.5	2.6	96.0	3.1	165.6	3.8	311.0	4.4	605.7	5.0

Note: Sales assumptions are based on the statement of corporate goals: 19X3, 30 percent increase; 19X4, 40 percent; 19X5, 50 percent; 19X6, 60 percent; 19X7, 70 percent.

Further assumptions are attained of over $10 billion in sales by the end of the fifth year and net income to be over 5 percent of net sales.

Source: Prepared by author.

By the same token, the amount of earnings is controlled by the number of shares and investment included in the goals section. If we have established further constraints, such as the ratios of net earnings to shareholders' equity and of net earnings to total assets, the payout ratio (dividends divided by net earnings), and the ratio of net earnings to tangible net worth, the projected range of net earnings will be narrowed even further.

Since we can establish a system of constraint equations, we can incorporate the changes required either manually or by using computers. Consequently, we can carry out strategic accounting analyses without undue effort, and within a reasonable time. Basically, the analyses involve a mix of historical accounting data and information supplied by top management. Thus, the numbers appearing on the financial statements may become normative and serve as guidelines.

In the next step, the feasibility and attainability of these figures should be examined. When the initial examination has been completed, we will be able to determine the attainability of each figure.

A very basic question remains to be resolved, intellectually. Are the problems of attainment due to limitations of tangible resources, or of intangible resources, including enthusiasm, effort, and intellectual capabilities? If we give up without anticipating the generation of alternatives and the possibility of innovation and creativity, we have taken a self-defeating approach.

For example, in order to attain the 70 percent increase in net sales in 19X7, the introduction of product Y in 19X3 (see Table 4.2) will help immeasurably, if the quality and price are sufficiently better than those of the competition to attract buyers. Even if the product is not outstanding, marketing strategy bolstered by aggressive advertising and promotion, attractive pricing, and vigorous sales maintenance strategy can be used to realize the net sales figures.

We have many alternative means by which we can attain the given ROI because it represents the outcome of multiplication of profitability rate by turnover rate, as shown in Figure 4.2; if we give each frontier line of the ROI, depending on the expected percentage of the ROI—such as 20 percent, 25 percent, or 30 percent—each line of the ROI is continuous. Thus, we can determine the best profitability and turnover rates if we are willing to spend enough time to identify each, or if we establish a mathematical model to discover the best combination.

In cases where we have no way to systematically establish the best combination, we must adopt a trial-and-error approach, which can be made more systematic if we preset the successive actions on the basis of a certain kind of response within given constraints. The better we can determine the major competitors' strategies in advance, the better we can make our in-depth analysis and preset a group of successive actions.

Thus, in the final step, we should come up with the most likely figures and tables, on the basis of which we can design and develop strategic packages. For this reason, the preliminary analysis should be made so as to minimize ineffectiveness and confusion in designing and developing the strategic packages.

A successful preliminary analysis should adjust and crystallize the broader and overlapping information into a more specific application ready for incorporation into strategic packages. The linkage aspect will be further clarified in the next section.

DESIGN OF STRATEGIC PACKAGES

Once the preliminary analyses have been completed, the next management procedure is to design and develop a group of strategic packages appropriate to each strategic (budgetary) unit.

1. Clarification of an independent project or task to be done by a strategic unit
2. Inclusion of the same items of information requirements as part of strategic planning shown in Figure 2.3
3. Adequate reflection of the linkage with other tasks or projects in the same or other strategic units
4. Inclusion of the credibility of information under the conditions of uncertainty, discontinuity, and turbulence.

The basic form and content of the strategic package, as shown in Figure 4.3, should reflect these statements.

First, each strategic package should include its name and number, the name of the strategic unit (and the relationship of the strategic unit to a group or a corporate unit, if necessary), the name of the director of the strategic unit, the level of the package (such as pessimistic/ most likely/ optimistic, or less necessary/ necessary/ very necessary), the date, and the name of the preparer. The name of the strategic package clarifies the nature and characteristics of the project or task that is further described in item (9). The statement should be concise, articulate, and consistent with previous materials and documents.

Second, the consistency of information requirements is checked by item (10) which includes a summary of the preliminary assessment. At least five points should be highlighted at this stage: checking to see if this package is designed with legal requirements in mind, or to agree with legislation anticipated in the near future; checking the net benefits summary in regard to the difference between total benefits and costs; making a competitive analysis summary; expected risks necessary to gain competitive advantages and to accomplish

TABLE 4.2. Product development, improvement, and abolition: Strategic planning, Unit A.

Nature of Products	First year	Second Year	Third Year	Fourth Year	Fifth year
1. New products					
a. HA product line					
(1) Product Y	P & S				
(2) Product Z	AS IN		P & S		
(3) Product X	FS		ES	CS	IN
(4) Product W	FS			ES	CS
(5) Product V	FS			ES	CS
b. IN product line					
c. PC product line					

68

2. Product improvement

a. Product A	improvement studies	production	sales	
b. Product B	improvement studies	production	sales	

3. Product abolition

	20%	50%		
a. Product E	product	reduction	rearrangement	abolition
b. Product F	product reduction	curtailment of production	rearrangement	abolition

P = product
S = sales
AS = application studies
IN = investment (facilities, other resources)
FS = feasibility studies
ES = engineering studies
CS = commodity studies

Source: Prepared by author.

FIGURE 4.2. Relationship between ROI and major financial indicators and accounting information.

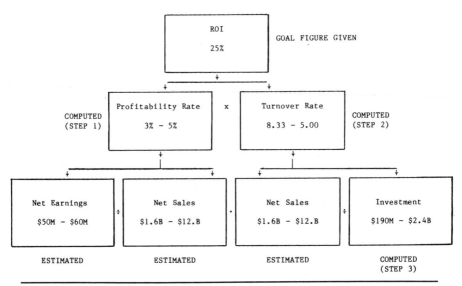

Source: Prepared by author.

the goals; and expected impact from and on other projects and strategic planning units. Through items (11) and (12), these aspects and additional ones can be examined in more detail for project feasibility, and direction of implementation and enhancement.

Third, the linkages with other projects and plans, specifically with the strategic plan, are accomplished by items (10), (17), and (18). In item (17), the cross-impact analysis is made by packages; and the number, name, and level of the strategic package are identified as those coming from other projects or strategic planning units, or as those going to other projects and strategic planning units. It is also important to assess secondary (indirect) or even tertiary impact should either threaten the strategic planning unit with heavy impact. These aspects will be discussed further in Chapter 5.

Fourth, items (12), (13), and (19) concern the probability of information. It is always wise to attach some form of probability information to each estimate. Since strategic budgeting is dynamic and multiple in nature, the level of the package indicates the range of selection. Using interval numbers may be another approach to dealing with uncertainty.[3] Credibility is subject to change as we gather more information. Therefore, these items should not be considered static, and changes should be reflected in them as soon as possible after the collection of new information.

FIGURE 4.3. Basic form of a strategic package.

(1)	(2)	(3)	(4)	(5)
Name of Strategic Package	No.	Name of Strategic Unit (SU)	Level	Priority

(6)	(7)	(8)
Name of SU Director	Prepared by:	Date

(9) Description;

FIGURE 4.3. *(continued).*

(10) Preliminary Assessment Summary:

(11) Reference Page No.

1. Is this package legislatively required? Yes _____ No _____

2. Net Benefits Summary: Total _____ Benefits _____ Cost _____

3. Competitive Advantages: _____ Low _____ Medium _____ High

4. Expected Risks Involved: _____ Low _____ Medium _____ High

5. Expected Impact Involved: _____ Low _____ Medium _____ High

(12) Quantitative Benefit Measures	19XX	19XX	This SP	Cumulative Total	19XX +1	19XX +2	19XX +3	19XX +4

(1)	(2)	(3)	(4)	(5)
Name of Strategic Package	No.	Name of Strategic Unit (SU)	Level	Priority

	19XX			19XX +1	19XX +2	19XX +3	19XX +4
(13) Tangible Resources Required	19XX	This SP	Cumulative Total				

73

FIGURE 4.3. *(continued).*

(14) Intangible or Descriptive Benefits:

(15) Intangible or Descriptive Costs:

(16) Consequences of Non-approval

 1. 25% Non-approval

 2. 50% Non-approval

 3. 75% Non-approval

 4. 100% Non-approval

(17) Cross Impact of this Package:

 1. From:

Package No.	Name	Level

 2. To:

Package No.	Name	Level

(18) Linkages to the specific strategic plan:

74

(1)	(2)	(3)	(4)	(5)
Name of Strategic Package	No.	Name of Strategic Unit (SU)	Level	Priority

(19) Contingency Plan:

   1. Conceivable Contingencies

      A. Man-made Contingencies   Probability   B. Natural Contingencies   Probability

   2. Possible Countermeasures

   3. Trigger Points

   4. Other Considerations

Source: Prepared by author.

Fifth, implementation and enhancement possibilities can be best incorporated via a rolling budget, so that the new year is added as the past fiscal year is deleted. However, the concept of the next five-year plan should be kept firmly behind the rolling plan, so that the important goals will remain intact and visible. Another means of increasing the flexibility is computerization. If the repetitive parts are computerized, we will have more time to spend on the aspects that demand creativity and individual treatment. This will both save time and give us more time for implementing and enhancing our present strategic budgeting system.

This illustrative package also includes items (14) and (15). We always need intangible and descriptive information to support the quantitative information. A decision based simply on surface numbers is likely to be misleading. Thus, we need to show the implications of the quantitative information.

Last, but not least important, the strategic package includes a contingency plan. This may be one of the most noteworthy differences between the strategic and decision packages in zero-based planning and budgeting. Since we must plan on a longer-term basis, a contingency plan is essential. Thus we have included item (19), which contains conceivable contingencies, possible countermeasures, establishment of trigger points, and other considerations, such as peculiar features or symptoms of contingencies and unique counteractions. The contingency plan may not have to be detailed year by year over the next five years. In this case, specific plans for before and after contingencies might be necessary in order to be able to make an effective evaluation of the most likely situations, both optimistic and pessimistic.

Consequently, in contrast with a decision package, a strategic package incorporates more long-term planning, an analysis of the credibility of information, and a contingency plan. In addition, more focused thinking should be devoted to the linkage with strategic planning units. The third aspect is the greater demand for creativity required for the strategic package than for the decision package.

Here again, it should be stressed that a strategic package by no means evolves discontinuously from a decision package. It should be viewed as an inevitable and sound outgrowth of the basic format, concepts, and techniques of zero-based budgeting. If the strategic planning function has not been developed in an overall planning system, then the strategic package may be a specific package in such an overall zero-based planning and budgeting system. On the other hand, if an elaborate strategic planning system has already been developed, a strategic package as well as a strategic unit should be developed and allowed to function independently, so that it may become the impetus for more strategic-planning-oriented zero-based budgeting systems (or strategic-planning-oriented PPBS).

The number of strategic packages in each strategic planning unit is subject to change, depending on needs and the level of sophistication of the project. Basically, however, there should be three: pessimistic, most likely, and optimistic. Because we must deal with uncertainties, discontinuities, and turbulence, it may not be sound to set up too many levels. The pessimistic level may (or may not) be the equivalent of the minimal level of effort and the optimistic level, of the maximum level of effort, in zero-based budgeting. If we establish another set of criteria—such as necessary for existence, present budget level, the optimum level—then the lowest level may coincide with the package having the minimum level of effort, and the highest with the optimum level.

What is really crucial in the strategic area is the feasibility and viability of planning. In other words, each strategic package should be achievable on a long-term basis rather than on a short-term basis. The minimal level is the minimum on a long-term basis, and is not necessarily the optimum or maximum on a short-term basis. This requirement is relevant when we classify decision packages into smaller decision packages.

Other aspects that must be considered are that each strategic package must be prioritized in some manner, and must be evaluated, ordinarily on two criteria: relative importance and the extent to which a package meets the objectives and goals of strategic planning. In general, more important packages will need more levels, in order to afford more in-depth evaluation, whereas less important packages may have fewer levels. As a result, important packages will probably be selected more frequently than less important packages, in terms of the number of packages appropriate to each strategic planning unit.

Since the chances of a strategic package's being approved hinge on an evaluation process in which the number of levels is important, in principle it becomes important that the number of levels is the same for each strategic package. More important, a strategic planning unit and a package should be designed so they include the same number of levels.

Still another aspect is that the minimal level in the strategic package is not always the minimal level in the sense that it is below the previous year's budget. Although such a situation may arise, the pessimistic level should not be set at the minimal level because the budget is far below the amount that will generate an incremental benefit over an incremental cost. If this situation is indicated, the choices are increasing the budget or terminating the strategic unit.

PRIORITIZING THE STRATEGIC PACKAGES

After completing the design of all strategic packages of the strategic unit, the fourth stage begins with the review of them. The ultimate objective of reviewing and prioritizing each strategic package is to accomplish the best allocation of limited resources. To the extent that the sum of resources required by all the strategic packages exceeds the amount of resources available, some method of resource allocation must be undertaken.

The method must be equitable, so that on a long-term basis, our strategic intention may be fulfilled in an effective manner. It is easier for the strategic package designer if the priority of the specific strategic plan is determined in advance. However, the more fully priority is delineated, the less chance there is of room for developing unique packages in a broader area. Consequently, it is usually desirable to leave some flexibility in specific identification and contents of the package.

There is a general rule for managing the ranking procedure. If many packages are to be evaluated and ranked, some kind of formal procedure must be instituted. If the number of packages is small, a more informal approach, such as discussions and formations of consensus on which are to be adopted, may be used.

In the latter case, ranking by an individual, such as the chief executive officer or vice-president for strategic planning, may be suitable. Since only one ranking is risky, ranking should be done at least twice, by different individuals. This depends, of course, on the size of the company and the extent of its growth and centralization. If the organization is growing rapidly, the evaluation and decision process should be minimized. In a state of maturity, a more participative and multiple method of evaluation will be valuable.

When many packages have to be ranked, two methods are most common: an executive evaluation committee or any central ranking committee, and voting. Both methods are frequently combined. Since discussions can be time-consuming, it is wise to establish guidelines for them. It is also necessary to understand that prioritizing does not always mean explicitly ranking. More frequently, at the initial stage only A, B, and C ranking, according to the extent of importance, is done. A might mean mandatory or very important, and C might mean not mandatory or less important. Once this sort of ranking is completed and three groups are tabulated separately, there is no need to evaluate packages in group A, except for a few that may cause concern over whether the total amount requested for them is within the range of the budget for the next year. Most efforts are usually concentrated on either B or C packages, particularly those around the cutoff line. If a cutoff line has been established somewhere in group C, a more detailed ascending or descending order must be established.

The popular six-point method or other scoring methods[4] may have to be used to arrive at the best mixture of objective scores and subjective judgment. As stressed before, in evaluating strategic packages (compared with decision packages) long-term net benefits are the most important. Therefore, sectional interests must always be subordinate to the attainment of an overall objective, as well as of specific strategic objectives.

In order to avoid the influence of sectional interests of evaluators who are representatives of one or more of the strategic planning units, a useful practice is to invite one or more outside evaluators to join in the process of ranking and evaluation. Such outside evaluators should, however, be well acquainted with the overall picture and interim details of the company. This method is often employed effectively in organizations in the public sector. Since ranking should be done from various perspectives based on a number of diverse viewpoints, experienced outside evaluation should in many cases be a requirement.

When outsiders participate, care must be taken to avoid leakage of confidential information. To do so, participation can be limited to the discussion stage, and voting or scoring can be done by inside committee members only.

In the author's experience with both zero-based and strategic budgeting, the initial ranking should by no means be the final one. Successive efforts using tabulating tables such as Tables 4.3 and 4.4 have helped greatly in uncovering the differences among evaluators, and have come up with better rankings through the consonance of their value judgments. In evaluating the crucial strategic package, such a preliminary ranking/discussion/reranking, a processs bolstered by the Delphi type of approach, is highly recommended. A more detailed, step-by-step approach will be shown in Chapter 6.

TABLE 4.3.   Strategic budget ranking analysis (1).

SPU	Project No.	No. Variance	Variance	Variance 1	Variance 2
Roasting	18	7 (39%)	11 (61%)	7 (39%)	4 (22%)
Vacuum	11	8 (73%)	3 (27%)	3 (27%)	0 (0%)
Institutional	3	2 (67%)	1 (33%)	1 (33%)	0 (0%)
Traffic	9	7 (71%)	2 (29%)	2 (29%)	0 (0%)
Soluble	8	4 (50%)	4 (50%)	4 (50%)	0 (0%)
Maintenance/ engineering	25	9 (36%)	16 (64%)	13 (52%)	3 (12%)
	74	37 (50%)	37 (50%)	30 (42%)	7 (9%)

Source: Prepared by author.

TABLE 4.4.   Strategic budget ranking analysis (II).

SPU	Project No.	Vice-President by 1	Manager by 2	Manager by 1	Vice-President by 2	Vice President: Manager
Roasting	18	7 (39%)	2 (11%)	2 (11%)	0 (0%)	7 (39%)
Vacuum	11	2 (18%)	0 (0%)	1 (9%)	0 (0%)	8 (73%)
Institutional	3	0 (0%)	0 (0%)	1 (33%)	0 (0%)	2 (67%)
Traffic	7	0 (0%)	0 (0%)	2 (29%)	0 (0%)	5 (71%)
Soluble	8	2 (25%)	0 (0%)	2 (25%)	0 (0%)	4 (50%)
Maintenance/ engineering	25	8 (25%)	2 (8%)	5 (25%)	1 (9%)	9 (38%)
	72	19 (26%)	4 (6%)	13 (18%)	1 (1%)	35 (49%)

Note: The numbers in columns 4 and 5 in Table 4.3 and columns 3 and 4 in Table 4.4 correspond to each other. They are the numbers of discrepancies in prioritizing the same project between vice-president and managers.

Source: Prepared by author.

Still another step is to specify the multiple voting criteria, as shown in Figure 4.4, even if the six-number or ten-point scale is consistently used. It is always possible to develop extremely detailed criteria, by use of which the most desirable allocation of weighting can be accomplished through voting. By continuously analyzing the extent of variance among the evaluators, we can come up with the desired degree of sophistication in the details of the evaluation and ranking criteria.

Basically, it is desirable to spend most of the time on the most important strategic package, and to allot successively smaller amounts of time to the second most important package and those ranked below it. In any case, sufficient time should be spent on discussion before voting is undertaken. The time to be allotted is also determined to some extent by the number of crucial packages. If two or more packages around the cutoff line are to be discussed, allocation of time for the discussions must be decided carefully.

A summary of the methods for prioritizing strategic packages is shown in Table 4.5 The subjective and objective methods, which basically represent a

FIGURE 4.4.   Multiple voting criteria.

1.   Legislative Requirements

Package may
be postponed

| 1 | 2 | 3 | 4 | 5 | 6 |

Package Required
to meet the Minimum
Legal Requirement

More Studies Required
↑

2.   Net Benefit Assessment

Net benefit
less than $10M
(or ROI < 10%)

| 1 | 2 | 3 | 4 | 5 | 6 |

Net benefit
exceeds $100M
(or ROI > 50%)

Net Benefit Exceeds $50M (or ROI > 25%)
↑
↑

3.   Risk Assessment

Probability of
risk loss is
much greater
than that of
package earnings

| 1 | 2 | 3 | 4 | 5 | 6 |

Probability of
package earning
much greater than
that of risk loss

Probability of loss due to risk equal to package earnings
↑

4.   Competitive Advantages
     (Self Market Share/ Major Competitor's Market Share)

Comparative
market share
less than 1.0.

| 1 | 2 | 3 | 4 | 5 | 6 |

Competitive; market
share exceeds 2.0

Comprehensive market share exceeds 1.5%
↑

5.   Impact Assessment

Impact to growth
of sales is
equal to or less than 1%

| 1 | 2 | 3 | 4 | 5 | 6 |

Impact to growth
in sales exceeds 10%

Impact to growth of sales is about 5%

Source: Prepared by author.

TABLE 4.5. Suggested methods for ranking strategic packages.

Subjective ranking	Individual ranking methods	single		evaluation (one-time ranking)
		double		evaluation (ranking on two separate occasions)
		multiple		evaluation (ranking more than twice)
	group ranking methods	open shop	voting methods	1-0 voting (yes or no)
				voting with scores (scoring method) with or without weighting
	group ranking methods	open shop	committee methods	discussion—consensus without Delphi method
				discussion—consensus with Delphi method
Subjective ranking	group ranking methods	closed shop	voting methods	1-0 voting (yes or no)
				voting with scores (scoring method) with or without weighting
	group ranking methods	closed shop	committee methods	discussion—consensus
				discussion—consensus check—discussion

Objective (semi-objective)	cost-effectiveness methods	incremental	incremental ratio approach incremental differential approach combination of above
Objective (semi-objective)	cost-effectiveness methods	absolute	total ratio (total effectiveness vs. costs) total difference (total effectiveness vs. costs) combination of the above
Objective (semi-objective)	industrial management	quantitative	industrial engineering approach (or systems analysis) management accounting approach (ratio, indices analyses, break-even analysis) financial management approach (capital budget, portfolio analysis)
Objective (semi-objective)	other disciplines	less quantitative	portfolio strategy approach (PPM, PIMS) information systems approach (value of information) other

Source: Prepared by author.

dichotomy, can be further classified. For example, the objective method should include some sort of scientific method, such as system analysis, cost-benefit analysis, or cost-effectiveness analysis. However, even in these analyses an absolutely objective analysis does not exist. Quantifications by no means assures an objective analysis of the problems we are attempting to solve.

For this reason, objective methods must be considered as comparatively objective or semi-objective. The use of concepts and techniques derived from statistical analysis may also be considered in prioritizing the strategic packages. Capital budgeting, financial management, and management accounting techniques are often partially or substantially utilized as part of the objective method.

Subjective methods are also varied. They may be further classified into open-shop and closed-shop methods, depending on the participation of outsiders. They are more often used as a means of group evaluation, compared with individual evaluation methods, which we have thus far discussed. As a result of ranking, we can complete a ranking table, as shown in Figure 4.5.

EXECUTION OF A STRATEGIC BUDGET

After ranking and reranking have been completed, the cutoff line set and approved strategic packages officially determined, then the strategic budget is executed. In the worst case, the necessity for change may arise soon after the budget is formally approved. It is necessary, therefore, to preplan methods of dealing with these changes. The changes in connection with the strategic planning unit, the strategic package, and other items will be discussed in Chapter 6.

Execution of the budget must be closely monitored, in terms of variances between actual and planned performances. However, essential differences do exist between the strategic budget and operational budgets and must be considered in evaluating these variances.

In the strategic budget, the variances that should get attention are those between planned performance and forecast performance, identified by the early warning system, whereas the variances between planned performance and actual performance are the major concern in the operational budget.

Second, in the operational budget the variance can, and should be, accurately measured in order to develop a feedback function that will help us to nullify or minimize future variances. Strategic budgeting, on the other hand, often will not require such a high degree of accuracy in an operational sense but, rather, the ability to see the differences in symptoms before the actual performance is measured. For this reason, we are required to measure prior variances by means of feedforward control.

Third, the operational budget is more structured and measured on a periodic basis, compared with the strategic budget. In general, the more successful the

85

FIGURE 4.5. Priority ranking table.

Strategic Planning Unit:	Group:	Prepared by:	Page ___
		Approved by:	Of ___

Strategic Packages			Current Year		Budget Year		
Priority	Human	$		Human Unit	$ (000)	Cumulative Human	Cumulative ($000)
Level	Unit	(000)		1 2 3 4 5	1 2 3 4 5	1 2 3 4 5	1 2 3 4 5
Rank	Name and Description						

Source: Prepared by author.

strategic budget, the more likely that operational budgeting will be in order. If strategic budgeting turns out to be unsuccessful, this will have a great impact on operational budgeting and may cause the operational budget to be totally infeasible. Therefore, successful monitoring of the strategic budgeting should precede the monitoring of the operational budget.

A vital question, then, is how we can successfully execute the strategic budget in connection with the early warning system. The answer to this question will depend on the quality and effectiveness of the early warning system, and the closeness of its relationship to the strategic budget. If the quality and effectiveness are very high, and the relationship between these two systems is very close, then the strategic budget has a much better chance of successful execution.

At this point, we will examine the nature of an early warning system. This sytem should have the capability of determining any situation that might cause risk to the achievement of the objectives of the firm at any time in the present or future. Not only must it be able to do this, but it must be able to detect the symptoms of any such situation in advance. Theoretically, the more varied capabilities we build into the system for doing this, the more likely we will be able to detect any indication of risk. Because of economic constraints, we normally cannot incorporate all the facilitites into the system that we would like, so we will be obliged to use to the fullest all the internal and external capabilities available for this purpose.

Thus, the development of sensitive external capabilities, and the sharpening of internal ones, is ordinarily the best we can do with the limited resources usually available. Clearly, the better we are at selecting more sensitive external detection capabilities, and at training internal ones to the highest levels of skill, the better our early warning system will be.

If we must use a consulting firm for external detection of threats, the performance record of the firm should be very carefully evaluated. Reputation alone does not justify selection of the outside firm. In technological forecasting, the person or group actually undertaking the forecasting is more important than the name of the company. Even a professional with a Nobel Prize to his credit should be carefully examined for recent performance.

Particularly in forecasting, the use of more highly sophisticated models does not guarantee greater credibility of results. A final decision should be made from among all the possible alternatives only after a careful examination of the record of each, and the reasoning behind the records, in the light of the most desirable internally established criteria.

In principle, every employee should become part of the detection system of the early warning system. Without such loyalty and willing cooperation, an early warning system cannot be established. Managers and executives should take the lead in establishing such a participatory early warning system. Cooperation and coordination between management and employees are essential for the establishment of a really workable early warning system.

Each employee should know in advance his or her role in the early warning system, and how important it is. Training for this purpose must be accomplished by cooperation between the manager and the employee. This must be a leader-follower relationship, but also an effective partnership formed to cope with unforeseen circumstances.

A stock purchase plan or some other sharing of the rewards may be necessary to provide needed incentives for full participation in difficult times. The keener the international competition becomes, the more the company needs to be a type of gemeinschaft rather than of gesellschaft.

Once such an early warning system begins to function effectively, it should become the basis of strategic planning and budgeting as well as of the contingency plan.

While we have stressed sensitivity in the early warning system, strategic budgeting should not be overly sensitive. Excessive sensitivity will cause serious problems in operational budgeting and, in the worst case, will make it impossible to execute operational budgeting in a routine and effective manner.

The strategic planning system should have enough resilience to protect it from being excessively influenced by disturbances. It should be equipped with a fail-safe system, so that inadvertent decisions and changes will not go through the system. To accomplish this, additional filtering criteria are needed in the crystallizing system.

There are many other subtle issues involved in executing the strategic budget. Some of these problems and considerations will be discussed in the ensuing chapters. In the final section of this chapter, we will summarize some suggested approaches and considerations for the successful institution of strategic budgeting.

SUGGESTED APPROACHES AND CONSIDERATIONS

First of all, the foundation must be firm and receptive to the new budgeting system. It is highly desirable for the company to have had some experience in either zero-based budgeting or program budgeting. If sound, long-term planning has already been established on zero-based budgeting, a natural outcome may be strengthening of strategic planning. On the other hand, companies that have developed an effective strategic planning system not coupled with an equivalent budgetary planning and control system should proceed to develop better linkage through the concept and techniques of strategic budgeting.

Second, it should again be noted that genuine enthusiasm and support by top management are essential. Since strategic budgeting is directly associated with the effectiveness of planning and control by top management, the leadership in instituting the new system must not be superficial or only partially participative. At every important point in the development of the budgeting system, the viewpoint and insight of the top management must be reflected. It is particularly important to bear in mind at this point the ten most important pitfalls to avoid in organizing and implementing long-range and strategic planning systems (as listed by Steiner).[5]

Third, strategic budgeting should reflect the quality and effectiveness of the strategic planning. In this respect, use of capable personnel is a key requirement. The personnel should be familiar with the general picture as well as the details of functions related to the nature of the products involved. In order to develop such personnel, an effective, long-range education and training program is essential. Those who design and develop the strategic budgeting system should not be professionals with limited backgrounds, such as accounting, finance, or engineering management, but people with experience and diversified backgrounds, familiar with the duties and responsibilities of each level of the organization.

Fourth, in companies still using a line-item-oriented budget with satisfactory results, do not try to develop a new budgeting system in areas where you believe the old one is functioning better than the new one will. If, however, you discover an excess of deficiencies over benefits in the old system, institute changes gradually. One way to do this is to make the first year an experiment; with two systems in operation; then, once you have confirmed that the merits exceed the demerits of the new system, gradually phase the old system out. It is also useful to introduce strategic budgeting in the area of capital budgeting, then enlarge its scope gradually.

Last, but not least in importance, it is essential that the new budgeting system be used as a means for building loyalty and increasing incentive in managers and employees, so as to develop enthusiasm and cooperative effort. Particularly in times of uncertainty, discontinuity, and turbulence, highly integrated effort in a results-minded climate makes it more likely that the company will be able to compete effectively. The institution of strategic budgeting, with the tools for effective thinking and planning that it provides, can often be the means of revitalizing both productivity and motivation, and thus of strengthening the company on a long-term basis.

NOTES

1. Cross-impact analysis will be discussed in Chapter 5.

2. Sidney Schoeffler, "Impacts of Business Strategy on Stock Prices," *The PIMSLETTER*, Strategic Planning Institute, 1980 no. 20, p. 1

3. For internal numbers, see Ramon E. Moore, *Interval Analysis* (Englewood Cliffs, N.J.: Prentice-Hall, 1966); and Akira Ishikawa, *Corporate Planning and Control Model Systems* (New York: New York University Press, 1975), pp. 105–17.

4. See Peter A. Pyhrr, "Zero Base Budgeting," *Harvard Business Review*, November–December 1970, pp. 116–18.

5. Among ten pitfalls, three are most conspicuous; they are: (1) Misconception by the top management on planning function that may be delegated to the planning section or staff, (2) Feasible goals are not established from the beginning, and (3) Inactive participation on the part of line managers in the process of establishing plans. According to Professor Toyohiro Kono's survey, (2) is equally conspicuous in Japan. For more detail, see George A. Steiner, *Strategic Managerial Planning*, The Planning Executive Institute, Oxford, Ohio, 1977. (Translated by Toyohiro Kono, *Senryaku Keiei Keikaku*, Diamond, 1978, pp. 130–138.)

Cross-Impact Analysis:
Definition and Significance
—5—

In Chapter 4, we did not touch on the cross-impact analysis, but merely mentioned it as one of the preliminary analyses to be made before preparing strategic packages. Because of its importance and significance, this chapter deals solely with that analysis. We will first define the cross-impact analysis; second, study its role in building a successful strategic package; third, outline the steps in completing an analysis; and fourth, give a few illustrations. Finally, we will explore the future directions of the cross-impact analysis.

DEFINITION OF THE CROSS-IMPACT ANALYSIS

Because of the increasing complexity and interrelationships that exist among the sections of modern organizations, particularly the technology-oriented firms, many kinds of prebudgeting—or, in broader terms, pre-resource allocation activities—are necessary. The crucial objective is to increase the effectiveness and efficiency of resource allocation. This should be accomplished by decreasing overlapping activities and by increasing the overall balance of our methods.

To decrease overlapping efforts, we must identify both the receivers of services and the suppliers who provide the services to a strategic unit. In other words, in preparing a strategic package, we must identify both inside-outside and outside-inside projects or tasks.

To achieve well-balanced and more concentrated results, we should identify indirect, as well as direct, services to and from the other strategic units. Thus we can determine to what extent our efforts are biased or too heavily concentrated on limited areas.

The cross-impact analysis is defined as a preliminary analysis to help all directors of strategic units identify and organize the essential and desirable interdependencies among their units. This exercise will determine and quantify what services will be included, how they will be provided, how often they will be provided, and who will provide them. Without this coordination and cooperation among strategic units, the effectiveness and efficiency of an overall service, as well as specific services, will be seriously impaired.

For example, if strategic unit B, responsible for new product X, has very few of the experts needed for this product but expects new experts to be hired, and strategic unit D, which is responsible for strategic units' personnel, has no plans to hire such experts, there is no way that strategic unit B can attain its basic objectives.

In this case, the requirements of strategic unit B must be communicated very specifically—how many experts must be hired, by what date, and what sort of qualifications they must have (or internal people must have) to qualify—to strategic unit D. In order to avoid such problems, each strategic unit should have the authority and responsibility to hire and dismiss the personnel needed. However, to the extent that the cross-impact analysis is effectively incorporated into the strategic budgeting process, it is possible to seek within the company personnel with the required qualifications, and to relocate employees as needed. This generally is more economical that hiring personnel from outside.

The purposes of the cross-impact analysis are to discover and to describe—if necessary, quantitatively—who does what for whom within the corporation in order to achieve effective strategic planning; to assess the extent of coordination and cooperation required among the strategic planning units; and to revise and implement the strategic package, should one be found to have an excessive burden compared with another package.

To attain these objectives, certain items should be included in a strategic package, and a summary table or figure designed to show cross-impact should be appended. In addition, appropriate criteria should be developed to determine excessive or insufficient cross-impact.

Thus, the role of the cross-impact analysis in designing and developing each package so that it meets both overall and specific strategic planning requirements is of great importance. Inasmuch as this analysis is new and not firmly established, there is plenty of room for evolution and development. This aspect will be further explored in relation to other analyses, such as cross-section analysis, in the final section of this chapter.

Even if clear, specific benefits from cross-impact analysis are not immediately obvious, by opening up communications on the common objective of strategic planning, the analysis will strengthen incentives and gradually increase the levels of cooperation and coordination that are so important in any organization.

BASIC STEPS OF CROSS-IMPACT ANALYSIS

Basically, three steps must be taken to complete a cross-impact analysis. The first is to identify all strategic planning units that will receive services from our strategic planning unit. We need to specify to these strategic planning units the kinds of services that we plan to supply, in terms of amount, frequency, quality, and associated costs, and to get their confirmation that these services will be adequate to enable them to execute their missions, duties, and responsibilities. If there are discrepancies between what we plan to supply and what they must receive, they should be adjusted as soon as possible.

The second step is to identify all strategic planning units that will supply services to our strategic planning unit. We then must specify to these units the services in terms of amount, frequency, quality, and associated costs that we expect to receive from them. If discrepancies exist between us and our suppliers, they should be adjusted as soon as possible.

The third and final step is to assure that no important differences exist, as suppliers, between us and the strategic planning units we supply, and, as receivers, between us and the strategic planning units from which we receive. If our strategic planning unit turns out to have an excessively large role as either supplier or receiver, its duties and responsibilities need to be reevaluated in order to avoid biasing the cross-impact analysis.

From beginning to end, cross-impact analysis requires close communication with other strategic planning units. At the first step, on identifying the projects and services to be supplied to other strategic planning units, we must receive confirmation that they are satisfactory. The services we intend to give and the services the receivers anticipate from us seldom coincide. Therefore, another approach is for us to receive their anticipations first, so that we can adjust accordingly. This can save time since, because we know their anticipations, we can make the adjustments with minimum conflict.

The same strategy can be applied to the second step. Before we receive the services to be supplied by other strategic planning units, we can issue a list of what we need. Thus they will be aware of our requirements, and therefore in a position to discuss any discrepancies with us.

In either step, while a simple adjustment can be accomplished by a short phone conversation, more complex adjustments require conferences. It may be helpful to show our plans, as a provider and as a receiver, in an established format, as shown in Figure 5.1, then hold formal meetings to consider areas where adjustments are needed. In cases of complicated issues, a judge or group of judges sent by headquarters may be required to resolve the conflict and, if necessary, a new mission for the strategic planning units may be identified.

There are several actions that can be taken to facilitate the execution of each step.

First, details and illustrations should be distributed as part of the guidelines for preparation of strategic packages. As each strategic unit director, or whoever is responsible for the cross-impact survey, receives more written forms and holds more informal conversations, the level of details usually becomes clearer and clearer. If the level of details is too high or too low, this is a signal to the strategic planning unit personnel that communications gaps exist, and efforts must be made to adjust the level in order to communicate effectively.

Second, language and definition gaps always occur. Therefore, care must be taken, particularly with respect to traditional expressions used by the different units. This problem can be greatly minimized by the issuance of a complete guidebook, with definitions of terms included, in preparation for putting together the strategic packages.

FIGURE 5.1. ABC International: Cross-impact analysis sheet.

To Receivers

To: SPU:

From: Director:

       Address

From: SPU:

To: Director:

       Address

Service we intend to provide	Volume	Frequency	Estimated Cost	Referral

FIGURE 5.1. (continued).

To Providers

To: SPU:

From: Director:

Address

From: SPU:

To: Director:

Address

Service we expect to receive	Volume	Required	Estimated Cost	Referral

TABLE 5.1. Summary of cross-impact analysis: ABC International.

						Decision Unit A
Receivers						
Services to be Provided						
Information Services Manager: Larry Carpenter	100	250 / 50	150 / 150		5200	
Personnel Manager: Charles O'Shea			100			80

TABLE 5.1. *(continued).*

	Decision Unit a
Suppliers/ (Providers)	
Services to be Received	
Product Development Manager: Larry Carpenter	60 35 55 75 90

Source: Prepared by author.

Note: The second Table highlights the names of the Strategic Units, while the first one does not contain them.

96

Third, a summary chart, as shown in Table 5.1, should be prepared so that services to be received and rendered can be specified. In addition, it is desirable to indicate priorities for both types of services. If a firm priority is established, the thrust of the discussions will be greatly clarified when discrepancies appear and resolution becomes difficult.

Finally, do not limit impacts to direct terms. We must also identify indirect impacts that are too significant to be ignored. For instance, if we ask for transfer of employees from another unit to ours, that unit will need to fill its vacancies from still another unit. This may set off a chain reaction in regard to important positions. In this case, hiring from outside may be more desirable, assuming that the incremental benefit exceeds the incremental cost. Also, care must be taken that a benefit from one unit does not result in a detriment to another unit. In the case mentioned, if the unit giving our unit the personnel cannot find suitable personnel from another unit, then the benefit to our unit has resulted in a detriment to another strategic planning unit. On an overall basis, through use of the cross-impact assessment, the total incremental benefit should exceed the total incremental costs.

SOME ILLUSTRATIONS

Let us continue to consider the case of ABC International. We will now assume it has reached the stage where it needs to make some sort of a cross-impact analysis before preparing strategic packages suitable for each strategic budgetary unit.

Larry Carpenter, director of strategic unit A, is now preparing to execute the form for cross-impact analysis. As indicated in Figure 5.1, there are two kinds of forms; one is to be filled in as a receiver of services and the other is to be filled in as a supplier of services.

He starts with the receiver's form in order to identify the services he needs to receive over the next five years—for example, from strategic unit P, information services. Since the basic responsibilities of Larry's unit are concerned with the marketing of old products as well as research and development of new products, he concludes that he needs all the information available on old and new products. His greatest concern is the marketing of similar products by major competitors before his company's product can be introduced.

For that reason, Larry also requests continuous information on what is going on in regard to similar products in other companies. He reasons that he needs access to rational data bases on research and development prepared by outside consulting organizations, in addition to information developed by his own efforts.

Second, product Y is now in field testing, prior to massive market introduction. Larry needs a statistical summary of the results of the field tests as soon as possible, so that additional study can be done by information services.

Third, Larry needs continuous retrieval of patent information related to new products in order to avoid the possibility of infringement, as well as to provide hints for the development of new ideas. Patent information services are available, but he feels it is important to study all the related patents, and that some of them might not be covered by the services.

Fourth, Larry wants collaboration in designing and developing effective project management and evaluation models related to the portfolio strategy models already developed. He has found it difficult to assess the effectiveness of research and development on an overall basis as well as for specific projects. Although specific project teams are organized for particular development tasks, he is not sure that each team is organized in the most effective manner and functioning efficiently, or at what point he should reorganize the teams if their effectiveness falls below expectations.

Last, Larry is beginning to feel very strongly that the information his unit receives is highly domestic. He wants more quality, worldwide information from information services. He realized over five years ago that his major competitors were foreign companies. In view of this competition, and greater investment in information services by competitors than by his own company, he feels that his company has not kept up in the techniques of use and development of international networks and systems. Larry realizes that information services really need to provide a number of additional services, but at this time he feels that the above are the five most important and urgent.

Now, Larry starts another receiver's form involving strategic unit L; personnel. He feels that he has many needs that this strategic unit can fulfill.

First, his unit is desperately short of first-class experts in the development of new products, and particularly for the development of product X. Although his own unit is already working on this problem, he feels that his need for an extensive search by personnel for experts on product X is most urgent.

Second, Larry has concluded that newspaper advertisements are not sufficient, and that personnel should greatly extend its activity in developing contacts with government and private agencies to find qualified personnel.

Third, Larry wants a list of qualified employees now in other strategic units. He has pointed out that relocating these talented people will result in greater benefits for the company as a whole. In order to assure this result, he requires a lot of additional information and a long-term personnel development program tailored to each individual.

Fourth, Larry feels that close ties with universities and colleges, particularly those with professors who can recognize and evaluate talent, are indispensable. He added this requirement because the past efforts of personnel have been too limited.

Finally, since he has not received either the original or a revision of strategic unit L's long-term employment and personnel development plan, Larry does not feel that he is in a position to ask for services that are most likely to be provided.

In any case, Larry feels that this may be the beginning of formal communication with other units. Up to now such communication has been limited to informal discussions that have deepened the conflicts and sharpened confrontations among the units of the organization.

Now, turning to strategic units to which services are to be rendered, Larry starts with the marketing services.

First, he feels very strongly that he should provide marketing services with the detailed plan and program of field experience with product Y. He will also include an initial plan for field testing of product Z.

Second, Larry realizes that he should include the introduction plan and program for improved products A, B, and C, so that marketing services will be in a position to provide the appropriate advertising and sales promotion. These plans clarify the number of personnel to be sent to work with market services personnel, and the length of time they will spend there.

Third, Larry reasons that complete marketing and sales promotion information, on new as well as present products, should be provided in order to make marketing of both types of products easier and more effective.

As he works on these forms, Larry begins to feel that they should be filled out from both the provider's and the receiver's viewpoints. This means that he must have a knowledge of all the activities throughout the entire company if he is to do the cross-impact analysis successfully.

As Larry goes on, he begins to realize the seriousness of the disorganization of the information function in the company, and becomes convinced that the cross-impact analysis will reveal the major part of the deficiencies, and serve as a good vehicle for designing and developing better-coordinated strategic packages.

Four illustrations of the cross-impact analysis are shown: two on the receiver's part, and two on the provider's part (Figures 5.2 through 5.5). These results are tabulated into a summary chart in Table 5.2. The level of details to be included in each column varies. Each service or task can be described by the priority order of the strategic planning units, or it can be written under a classification system such as basic services vs. applied services, or primary services, secondary services, and so forth. For each service element there is a reference number or page number of the prepared document. Some of the more important reference numbers may be written in red ink or marked with an asterisk.

By reviewing a summary of the cross-impact analysis, we can detect any overlapping or overlooked services or tasks. In addition, the level of detail and crystallization can be examined on an overall basis.

One of the important aspects to be examined is whether a service provided is in fact utilized, and how the service will affect other services. While some services have a marked tendency to cause chain reactions, many others do not. Essentially, we must try to provide services that will result in great benefit not only to the receiver but also to the receiver from the receiver, and so on. We look into this requirement in the next section.

FIGURE 5.2. Cross-impact analysis: Receiver's side.

To:

Strategic Unit P: Information Services

Manager: John Wisdom

Address: Second Floor - Building G-2

From:

Strategic Unit A: Project Development

Manager: Larry Carpenter

Address: Tenth Floor - Building G-2

In preparing our strategic packages, we have identified your Unit as a provider of services to our Unit. Details follow.

Service we expect to receive	(Amount) Volume	(Duration) Frequency	Estimated Cost	Referral
1. To arrange access for us to outside data bases on R&D	2 hours per day	Once a week	100	P-5
2. A statistical summary of field tests in progress	1 volume	Once	250 50	P-6
3. Retrieval of patent information on new products	4 hours per day	3 days per month	150	P-12
4. Design and development of product management and evaluation models	8 hours per day	6 months	1500	P-15
5. Development of international information network and systems	6 hours per day	3 years	5200	P-30

Source: Prepared by author.

FIGURE 5.3. Cross-impact analysis: Receiver's side.

To:

Strategic Unit L: Personnel

Manager: Charles O'Shea

Address: Fourth Floor — Building G-3

From:

Strategic Unit A: Project Development

Manager: Larry Carpenter

Address: Tenth Floor — Building G-2

In preparing our strategic packages, we have identified your Unit as a provider of services to our Unit. Details follow.

Service we expect to receive	(Amount) Volume	(Duration) Frequency	Estimated Cost	Referral
1. To hire a first-class expert to develop varied new products, particularly product X	1-2 persons		100	P-17
2. To interface with national and private institutes and employment agencies to find talented personnel	2	As often as possible	80	P-33
3. To provide us with a list of employees in other units	2	Once a year	50	P-34
4. To establish better communications with colleges and universities, particularly through professors	10-20	Twice a year or more	50	P-40
5. To supply us with an original and revised long-term employment and personnel development plan	1 of each	Once a year	150	P-45

Source: Prepared by author.

FIGURE 5.4. Cross-impact analysis: Supplier's side.

To:

Strategic Unit M: Marketing Services

Manager:　　　Ted Spinkle

Address:　　　Third Floor 1-4 — Building G-4

From:

Strategic Unit A: Project Development

Manager:　　　Larry Carpenter

Address:　　　Tenth Floor — Building G-2

In preparing our strategic packages, we have identified your Unit as a receiver of services from our Unit. Details follow.

Service we intend to provide	(Amount) Volume	(Duration) Frequency	Estimated Cost	Referral
1. To provide you with complete detailed plan and programs on the field experiments of Y	2	3 months	150	P-48
2. To provide introductory plan on improved products A, B, and C	1	Within a year	50	P-50
3. To provide all sorts of marketing and sales information on new products	3	Twice per year	75	P-52
4. To provide all sorts of marketing and sales promotion information on improved products	3	Three times per year	45	P-57
5. To provide additional information, if any, to help accomplish better marketing services	Not decided	As often as possible	Not decided	P-60

Source: Prepared by author.

FIGURE 5.5. Cross-impact analysis: Supplier's side.

To:

Strategic Unit M: Personnel

Manager: Charles Oliver

Address: Fourth Floor — Building I-2

From:

Strategic Unit A: Project Development

Manager: Larry Carpenter

Address: Tenth Floor — Building G-2

In preparing our strategic packages, we have identified your Unit as a receiver of services from our Unit. Details follow.

Service we intend to provide	(Amount) Volume	(Duration) Frequency	Estimated Cost	Referral
1. Interface with professional meetings and conferences to find talented candidates for new product development	Not decided	As often as possible	60	P-10
2. Our long-term personnel development and educational plan	1	Twice a year	35	P-75
3. Professional seminars and meetings we have to participate in	1	Once a month	55	P-80
4. Business shows, science and technology Exhibitions in which we have to exhibit	2	One week each	75	P-85
5. Business shows, science and technology Exhibitions we must see	4	Once in 6 months	40	P-90

Source: Prepared by author.

TABLE 5.2. Summary of cross-impact analysis: Decision unit A, ABC International.

Services to be Provided Receivers	Detailed Plan of Field Experiments. Product Y	Introduction Plans. Products A. B. C	Marketing Sales Promotion Information on new Products	Marketing Sales Promotion on Improved Product	Additional Sales and Promotion Information	Interface with Professional Meetings and Conferences	Long-Term Personnel Development Plan	*Professional* Meetings, Seminars, Business Shows, Science and Technology Exhibitions
Strategic unit M marketing services	48	50	52		57	60		

Source: Prepared by author.

FUTURE DIRECTIONS OF CROSS-IMPACT ANALYSIS

There are several directions in which the present state of cross-impact analysis can be improved, within the framework of one of the preliminary analyses for strategic budgeting.

One of the most important is to set up a system of evaluation to enable us not only to detect overlapping and redundancy of services and tasks, but also to assess the nature of the services to be provided. The issue is not the number of services to be provided, but how many of the services are really needed. The need for services provided may be different at different times in one strategic planning unit, and different at the same time among different strategic planning units.

The second direction is to explore the secondary and tertiary effects of one service. It is entirely conceivable that a service that has a rather weak initial impact may have subsequent impacts that are much stronger, while another may have a more substantial initial impact, but have no noticeable subsequent impacts. For example, a rise in raw material costs may have little effect at the level of the initial buyer, but a greater impact at the wholesale level, even more at the retail level, and become great at the consumer level. Such a situation depends on the level of development in the country. The sudden rise in petroleum costs may not affect well-developed countries nearly as much as developing and undeveloped countries. Generally, the impact on less-developed countries will directly affect their social, economic, and military development. Large multinational companies will be less affected than medium-size or small companies, although the direct effect will depend largely on the use of petroleum.

The third direction of development is the provision of more data developed from many angles. For example, as shown in Fugure 5.6, the coefficients based solely on prior interlocking structures denote the relative extent of impacts in order to predict the cash operating ratio. However, this is only one group of coefficients and variables, and it can be related, if necessary, to additional dependent variables. Another approach is to break down one independent variable or dependent variable into sub-variables. This process may be developed into the identification of sub-subvariables, so that we can quantitatively analyze how the inital impact will be passed on. By doing so, we will be able to determine the effects of successive impacts.

The fourth direction is to find the desirable relationship with similar analyses, such as cross-section analysis or multi-dimensional analysis.

In a broader sense, cross-impact analysis may be considered a part of cross-section analysis. While cross-section analysis deals with the comparative analysis between or among different sections or entities, it deals with the degree of impact in cross-section, whatever methods of analysis may be used. Cross-section has the specific meaning of comparing two different bodies of factors yet to be analyzed. It also means looking at something from different angles.

FIGURE 5.6. Equations concerning cash: Operating ratio, illustrating three strategic analyses.

Coincident Indicators (found in Budget and "What...if" Structures):	Budget (From Figure 1)	Types of Analysis		Forecasting Based Solely on Prior Interlocking Structure
		"What...if" Forecasting	"What...if" Forecasting	
Accumulated depreciation divided by flight equipment at cost (1949-71)			-.13	-.10
Depreciation cost			-.17	
Number of employees at year end (1952-72)				-.27
Revenue passengers as % of industry total (1952-74)		-.59		-.47
Miles per average scheduled ticket (1952-74)				+.94
Available seat miles (1952-74)			-.10	
Revenue passenger miles divided by passenger aircraft at year end (1952-74)		+.14		
Revenue passenger miles divided by wages, nonretirement benefits (1952-74)			-.13	
Scheduled passenger load factor (1953-75)		-.43		-.39
Revenue passengers as % of industry total (1953-75)		-.24		

Leading Indicators (Found in "What...if" Forecasts and Forecasts Based Solely on Prior Structures):	Budget (From Figure I)	Types of Analysis	
		"What...if" Forecasting	"What...if" Forecasting Based Solely on Prior Interlocking Structure
Wages, nonretirement benefits (1954-76)			-.60
Revenue per passenger mile as % of industry average (1954-76)		-3.07	
Passenger revenue divided by passenger aircraft at year end (1954-76)	+.40		
Revenue passengers as % of industry total (1954-76)	+.56		
Personnel at year end (1954-76)	+.47		
Depreciation on flight equipment (1954-76)	+.23		
Flight equipment at cost (1954-76)	+.19		

Source: Reprinted, by permission of the publisher from Edmund J. Luksus, "Strategic Budgeting: How to Turn Financial Records into a Strategic Asset" Management Review, March 1981 p. 60,©1981, by AMACOM, a division of American Management Associations. All rights reserved.

111

Therefore, in many cases cross-section analysis leads to the identification of some sort of quantitative relationship among sections—for example, the productivity indices of plants A, B, and C or of steel, automobile, and electronics industries—as well as of the relative impacts on these sections. Another function of the cross-impact analysis is to identify—quantitatively, if possible—the nature of the force that transmits the impacts. This may be better explained by adopting the cybernetic approach.

The fifth and last direction is to supplement the quantitative analysis with some sort of qualitative or behavioral analysis. Since all of the direct and indirect impacts may not be identified, quantitative descriptive or behavioral approaches may be required. The extent of impact may be explored to some extent by use of questionnaires and interviews.

The focal point will be the matching of service receivers and suppliers at the same level of cognition and understanding. If receivers fail to discern the same level of cognitive impacts that providers discern, the cross-impact analysis will not be successful. Further, the intent of the issuer of the impact should be accurately read and conveyed to the successive receivers, and it should be done continuously.

Care must be taken to ensure that the contents of the impact are not disguised or distorted, since it is very difficult to convey a real intent from one receiver to another in an accurate manner. For this reason, continuous evaluations should be made. In addition, once the nature of an impact is changed, that change should be transmitted without delay.

Transition and Implementation
of Strategic Budgeting

——6——

Inasmuch as there are always problems in forecasting sales, net profit, or any other major figures or indices, we should be ready to deal with all possible changes in the foreseeable future.

For example, a change in strategic planning within a fiscal year should always cause a change in the strategic budget. Even if no major changes occur, a minor change will cause changes in the strategic units within a budgetary year. Or, assuming that a strategic unit disappears within the fiscal year, the change of strategic packages within the budgetary year may be inevitable. We intend to explore these changes, from major to minor.

CHANGE OF STRATEGIC PLANNING WITHIN A FISCAL YEAR

Many changes are possible, running the gamut from total overhaul or alteration of the strategic planning concepts and procedures to a very minor change in part of the procedure of strategic planning.

For example, changes in environmental forecasts, opportunity and threat, strength and weakness, and analysis of products will all cause change in the strategic budgeting. In like manner, new ventures, mergers, acquisitions and divestments, a new sales program, and implementation of processes and procedures will affect strategic budgeting. Some of them affect both strategic units and packages, while others affect strategic packages only. Changes in viability and profitability programs will also cause changes in the strategic packages, either in whole or in part.

For example, if a recession is predicted to last nine months longer than the original forecast, this environmental forecast change will directly affect sales, and then production planning, material purchases, inventory, the labor force, and, eventually, net profit. This will not be the end. Lower net profit will result in lower investment, and vigorous long-term investment may be discontinued.

If, because of international competition, top management attempts to continue vigorous long-term investment, some tangibles such as facilities, machinery and equipment, and labor force may have to be sacrificed, in absence of other alternatives. However, the reduction in labor force should be the very final step. Before making this decision, there are many other avenues to be explored. This is particularly true in areas where other jobs are not available except for those with special skills.

Typical strategies range from decreasing inventories and excessive numbers of forms and documents, to being merged or acquired. Even when forced to lay off workers, many Japanese companies use a stage-by-stage approach. They first reduce the bonuses of the executives and managers, and then the reductions are spread to the rest of the workers. If this is insufficient, then they put into effect a plan of increasing reductions in wages and salaries, paying 90 percent, 75 percent, 50 percent, and so on.

Even if there is no job for them, some employees are still retained by the company. If no regular production can be scheduled, then a certain percentage of the employees are asked to await a resumption of production at home but are not laid off.

Relocation is another alternative. In a well diversified company, while one division may be losing money, another may be increasing its profit. Unless all or a substantial number of the divisions of the company are losing money, relocation in many cases can solve even the worst problem.

For example, assume that as a result of a recession, a production plan must be reduced by 30 percent. The result will be, first of all, a reduction in the labor force. This will affect other functions, such as marketing, finance, personnel, and public relations, and eventually will be felt in R&D. Therefore, production-related strategic units may be reduced or eliminated. This will naturally be reflected in the contents and selection of the decision packages.

Long-term budget levels will decline, or the optimistic and most likely levels will be dropped in the process of choosing an acceptable group of strategic packages. The worksheet for increasing or decreasing the budget and the change of a cutoff line are shown in Table 6.1

CHANGE OF STRATEGIC UNITS WITHIN A BUDGETARY YEAR

The case in which all or some of the strategic units must be changed is best represented by the reorganization required by discontinuous change of strategic planning. Let us consider several likely cases.

Alternative 1 is the case of total change. For instance, a change from the traditional, functional organization to the business- or product-line-oriented organization is being considered in order to incorporate the strategic budgeting system.

In this case, the change is substantial. Each functional department, such as production, marketing, or sales, is segmented by product or business line and will become the production, marketing, or sales function for product A, B, or C or business A, B, or C. Therefore, this case may be regarded as a birth of the strategic units rather than the change of strategic units. One example of change of strategic units is that in which a company changes from the textile to the computer industry—that is, from a declining industry to one with brighter prospects. In this case, even if the business has already adopted the business-line-oriented organization, the change is still substantial. A complete reorganization should be carried out.

Alternative 2 is the case of a partial change. There are many such cases, usually resulting from adding or deleting a product or business line. If an automobile company decides to add a word-processing business and reduce the number of unprofitable lines, changes will be limited to the lines that are being added or eliminated. Within these lines, however, substantial changes may be needed.

Realistically, it will be difficult to get workers used to working on automobiles to adapt to word-processing equipment quickly, unless conversion procedures and training programs have been carefully worked out and are enforced. New strategic units might be designed by the top expert in the word-processing equipment field, working with his counterpart in the automobile manufacturing area. If the work force is predominantly young, it will probably be more adaptable than if composed mostly of older workers.

In the second case, the following steps must be taken:

1. Identify the appropriate number of strategic units by unique and independent business lines
2. Distinguish those strategic packages that need to be revised from those packages that do not
3. Distinguish further between those packages that need to be completely or substantially rewritten, and those that do not need much revision.

It is best to start with those strategic units and packages that need complete change. Even the number and format of strategic packages may change as a result of the emergence of completely new strategic units.

Upon completing the identification of the missions, duties, and responsibilities of those strategic units that need substantial change, we can go on to the strategic units that require a more modest change, and end with the strategic units that need the least change.

The fact that some strategic units need little change does not mean that the changes in the strategic packages will be correspondingly small, particularly in cases where a new objective is added that is completely independent of other objectives.

For example, at the transition stage, strategic unit P may need to cover both the new automobile Q and the new word-processing machine R. Since the natures of these products are quite different, addition of a new product line requires the production of completely new strategic packages—possibly more packages than required for the automobile. Particularly if we intend to manufacture several models of the word-processing machine, establishing the most effective combination of executive and strategic centers will call for a large number of strategic packages.

TABLE 6.1 Midyear budget implementation: Alternative changes (based on change of the midyear budget from $10,530,000 to $9,650,000; budget and cumulative figures in thousands of dollars)

Rank	Name of Strategic Package	19X3 Proposed		Budget	19X2 Cumulative % of 19X2 Revised
		Positions	Budget		
81	Basic research—VLSI	5	150	7,380	100
82	Production, development lasers, solid state	3	300	7,680	
83	Basic research—individual enzymes (6 of 12)	7	350	8,030	109
84	Personnel development program C (4 of 6)	2	60	8,090	
85	Information services program D (3 of 5)	10	400	8,490	
86	Production and development interferon (7 of 12)	5	250	8,740	118
87	Applied research, gene synthesizer (6 of 25)	8	700	9,440	
88	Management project L (9 of 51)	3	150	9,590	
89	Personnel development program D (5 of 6)	2	60	9,650	131
90	Merger and acquisitions, analysis V (6 of 7)	11	500	10,150	
91	Information services program E	9	200	10,350	
92	Productivity enhancement program (7 of 8)	4	180	10,530	143
			3,300		

TABLE 6.1. (continued)

Worksheet 1 Effective Reduction Remainder of Year			Worksheet 2 Effective Reduction Remainder of Year			Worksheet 3 Effective Reduction Remainder of Year				
Rank	Budget	Cumulative	Rank	Budget	Cumulative	Rank	Rate (1)	(1) 19X0	Budget	Cumulative
81	7,380	100	81	77	7,307	81	.045	40	110	7,340
82	7,680		82	227	7,534	82	.091	80	220	7,560
83	8,030	109	83	277	7,811	83	.106	93	257	7,817
84	8,090	118	84	0	7,811	84	.018	16	44	7,861
85	8,490		85	327	8,125	85	.121	106	294	8,155
86	8,740		86	177	8,302	86	.076	67	183	8,338
87	9,440		87	627	8,929	87	.212	187	513	8,851
88	9,540		88	77	9,006	88	.045	40	110	8,961
89	9,650	131	89	0	9,006	89	.018	16	44	9,005
			90	427	9,420	90	.152	134	366	9,371
			91	127	9,545	91	.061	54	146	9,517
			92	77	9,650	92	.055	47	133	9,650
Alternative 1 Simply cutting off			Alternative 2 Across-the-board reduction			Alternative 3 Proportionate change by strategic package				

117

TABLE 6.1. (continued).

Worksheet 4
Effective Reduction Remainder of Year

Rank	Required Change	Budget	Cumulative	Notes:
81	30	120	7,350	Alternative 1 is a case of simple cutting off at the level of $9,650,000. This level is an increase of 131% in comparison with the previous year's budget. Alternative 2 shows across-the-board reduction in the amount of $73,000. Consequently, basic research—VLS 1 (rank 81) becomes $150,000 − $73,000 = $77,000, as shown in row 1, and information services program (rank 85) becomes $400,000 − $73,000 = $327,000, as shown in row 5.
82	90	1,210	7,460	
83	100	250	7,810	
84	20	40	7,750	
85	90	310	8,060	
86	30	220	8,280	Alternative 3 indicates the proportionate reduction by strategic packages. For example, basic research (rank 81)'s share on the same page is $150,000/$330,000 = .0245. This number appears on the first row in the rate column. Since we have to reduce by $880,000 ($10,530,000 − $9,650,000), $880,000 × 0.045 = $40,000 is the amount to be reduced. Thus, the budget on rank 81 becomes $110,000, shown in the first row in the budget column.
87	210	590	8,870	
88	40	110	8,980	
89	20	40	9,020	
90	150	350	9,370	
91	40	160	9,530	
92	60	120	9,650	

Alternative 4

Reexamination of each strategic package

Generally the importance and potential of the objective require execution of many diversified missions and the establishment of many responsibilities, which of course will increase the number of strategic packages for any given business line. However, as stressed previously, the number of strategic packages should not be too great, or their nature too varied. Control should basically be maintained over the number of strategic units rather than strategic packages.

It is always desirable to design the transition of strategic units and the respective packages in advance, so that reworking, and the time spent doing so, can be avoided.

TRANSITION OF STRATEGIC PACKAGES WITHIN A BUDGETARY YEAR

Changing the strategic packages is the simplest change to make. To the extent that no change in format is required, we can rewrite the contents of each strategic package and transfer it to a ranking table so that reranking can be carried out.

Where we must substantially change the contents of strategic packages, it is quite likely that a complete reranking will have to be done. The greater the change of the contents of the strategic packages, the greater the likelihood of the need for complete reranking. Very minor changes of the strategic packages, on the other hand, may require no reranking at all.

While adding new businesses or deleting ongoing business lines may be expected to change the contents of strategic packages, increases or decreases in the budget will certainly affect both the content and the number of strategic packages that will be approved. Since most situations are subject to change, in many cases we will have to rewrite established strategic packages when the budget is changed. Of course, the establishment of more alternative packages than required at the outset can help solve this repetitive and time-consuming problem.

The steps to be taken in the change of strategic packages following budget revisions are the following:

1. Develop new strategic packages, if needed, to meet requirements not presented in the previous budget
2. Revise the strategic packages if the needs of the organization differ significantly from the premises of the strategic planning on which the packages were originally developed
3. Modify the rankings to make them consistent with any changes in the priorities, including both the new and revised strategic packages
4. Once the strategic budgeting analysis has been completed:
a. Eliminate originally funded strategic packages, beginning with the lowest priority, up to the point where the desired level is reached, or
b. Add unfunded strategic packages, old, revised, or new, beginning with the highest priority, up to the piont where the additional funds are exhausted.

Note that in the process of ranking, we must consider three packages: entirely new, revised, and old or unchanged.

REQUIRED TASKS FOR IMPLEMENTATION AND EVOLUTION

In order to implement the strategic budgeting system once it is established, we must evaluate the merits and demerits as they actually occur, and compare them with our planned, or anticipated, merits and demerits. This should be done periodically, at fixed times. If the actual results are not impressive when compared with the anticipated results, a serious examination would be made of the following:

1. Feasibility of the total framework of strategic budgeting
2. Design and development of the process and procedure
3. Correctness of management procedures and strategic budgeting
4. Pertinence of evaluation criteria.

In the early period of introduction of a new budgeting system, benefits may not be quick to appear, and deficiencies are often overstated. Therefore, it is very desirable to follow through on the points mentioned above by organizing an appropriate implementation and review task force.

First of all, with respect to the feasibility of the total framework of strategic budgeting, the process introduced in Chapter 2, particularly Figure 2.2, should be recalled. The question is whether the strategic planning and budgeting system is applicable to our company at our level of budgeting. If it is not, another system should be developed. If it is applicable and reasonable, then we will be able to examine each block of the system or information flow diagram and follow the flow from block to block.

For example, we have to consider the following questions in connection with the block of premises:

1. Do we have adequate means—models and specialists—to realistically forecast our future environment?
2. Have we sufficiently identified the opportunities and threats? If so, can we continue to do so adequately in the future?
3. Have we adequately analyzed product and business lines that can be reflected in strategic budgeting? If so, can we maintain the same level of adequacy in the future?
4. Have we identified the correct and workable differences between what should be done and what can be done? If so, can we maintain the same level of discrimination in the future?
5. Have we everything necessary to formulate an effective strategic plan?

Second, the audit and examination of the process and procedure should be undertaken on an input-output approach. We must identify who does what task in what manner, and from whom and in what manner one receives information needed to transmit intelligence (processed information) to whom. The intelligence may be documents on environmental forecasts, opportunities and threats, analysis of products, new venture analysis, merger and acquisition analysis, or shift of product mixes report, for instance.

What is really important in this case is to find out whether what was established as the process and procedure has been followed, where there are deficiencies, and how to implement correction of these deficiencies. In addition, simplification of the means of attaining the original or higher levels of efficiency should always be considered.

By means of word-processing devices, tables, figures, forms, and statements can be stored and easily retrieved when needed. This easy availability offers tremendous advantages in avoiding the waste of man-hours on repeating the same job over and over. If we wish to use such systems, we can, for instance, retrieve the detailed system flow chart as well as an overall system diagram. As we accumulate more information, we will learn to differentiate the more important information and the resultant output from that of less value.

Third, examination of the management procedure of strategic budgeting requires time and attention to determine if it is, in fact, feasible and workable. If we have established a set of criteria for evaluation and implementation in advance, we will be able to take action more promptly. We must take care, however, not to make superficial decisions while we are still not familiar with the significance of the previously established management procedure. Longer study and experience are required to understand some management procedures than others.

For example, ranking may take much more time than constructing strategic packages. In order to reduce the time required, we can introduce A, B, and C ranking or a form of less hierarchical ranking. What is most important is to come up with an unbiased and effective ranking, whatever the system used. If simplification threatens the accuracy of the ranking, then of course we must not incorporate the simplified system as a possible alternative.

Finally, examination of the evaluation criteria is most important, even though it is most difficult. We tend to forget subsequent action once we have established a set of evaluation criteria. We can set up both overall and specific criteria. If the criteria are too "overall" and abstract, they cannot be considered pertinent. On the other hand, if they are too specific, they are not appropriate either.

In many cases "strategic budgeting should be effective" is one of the criteria we tend to establish. However, it is not very enlightening. The effectiveness must be explained in a more concrete manner, such as "strategic budgeting should be effective enough to give top management twice as much strategic information as given by our traditional budgeting or zero-based budgeting." In this case "strategic information" means information of strategic value to its user.

Tasks required for implementation and development are in principle both unique and innovative. In other words, the more completely we are surrounded by an environment in which innovation and invention are fostered, the more we will be able to identify the tasks required for implementation and development. As soon as we become content with the present status, we are unable to conceive any tasks for implementation. Therefore, to maintain constant implementation, each employee must be adventurous, full of curiosity, and of an innovative mind and spirit.

The real focal point is how to maintain such a frame of mind and spirit among all members of the corporation on a long-term basis. Education and training should be made more effective, and appropriate setting of objectives and leadership must be provided by the head of the company.

RELATIONSHIP BETWEEN STRATEGIC BUDGET AND TECHNOLOGICAL BREAKTHROUGH

There can be no doubt that a successful technological breakthrough can be of great help in implementing strategic planning. As mentioned before, a continuously innovative state of mind is the key to implementation and enhancement of any system. This is even more the case as the competition becomes keener.

For example, if you are starting to be successful in automatic gene synthesizers, which are entirely new products, the direction of the implementation of strategic budgeting may have to change entirely, perhaps heading in the direction of effectively repositioning product mixes, and determining how long it will take the automatic gene synthesizers to become "cash cows." As a result, a new product mix model or a more detailed strategic process model may have to be created.

What is really important, however, is successful interpretation of the overall trend and thrust of biotechnological research. If your company is a precursor in the related technology, and if another country, such as Japan, has taken up biotechnology as a major industry for the future and has initiated a ten-year, $100 million program sponsored by one of the government agencies, the results of these aggressive research efforts should be carefully monitored.

It may be easy for you to determine in what areas how much investment must be made, and what companies will enter each area, such as recombinant DNA, bioreactor development, and large-scale cell growth. Research will tell you what companies will require the basic technology and also what the future of research in that area of biotechnology will be.

In order to follow the progress of other companies, a strategic information center is inevitable. For example, while Japanese companies deploy 1,500 software experts on the information systems in the United States, supported by a budget of $25-$30 million per year, American industrial intelligence in Japan is virtually nothing.[1]

However skillful product-cycle analysis or portfolio analysis may be, without massive research on a group basis at government initiative, international competition will never be successful on a long-term basis. Exchange of product development costs and related information is vital to linking strategic budgets with technological breakthroughs.

Since technological breakthrough is accomplished by a mixture of fundamental and applied research, strategic budgeting should be based on discovering the most desirable mixture, rather than allocating a specific R&D budget to each project. Special care must be taken to refine the methods by which we measure strategic expenditures (as differentiated from operational expenses).

This is because of the nature of the costs, which should not be eliminated carelessly in a period of economizing, even if revenue to cover them is not yet clearly anticipated. Consequently, basic research generally should be assessed on a longer-term basis than applied or engineering research, which is usually assigned on a short-term basis. This means that strategic budgeting for basic research requires greater insight and creativity than that for applied research.

Exploration, creativity, and discovery in every area should be continuous, paralleling ongoing research and development. If we could develop a large enough data base on creativity and innovation to design and develop a computer-based creativity evaluation model,[2] it would be a great help in identifying the pertinent areas of basic research, and would be useful for evaluating the ongoing, applied research and development.

The objectives of this sort of model are to find the most appropriate group of products, based on both overall and specific analyses of the company; to find the shortest time and route from start to completion of a new product; to detect inefficiency and ineffectiveness inherent in the research and development process; and, above all, to construct the budget so that the most effective mix of fundamental and applied research can be carried out.

In basic research, in the extreme case where no relevant information is available, the budget amount will be controlled by the kinds of information and equipment to be used; by the frequency of attending professional meetings, conferences, and symposia; and by royalties, licensing fees, and related activities.

If, however, a discovery or invention occurs, determining the feasibility of its commercialization will become the main concern, and the budget will have to be substantially changed. At this point, strategic budgeting should normally be changed in a discontinuous manner. In other words, if further basic research is judged not to be cost-effective, the transition from basic to applied research and development should be made in the implementation process of strategic budgeting.

One quantitative analysis of research and development strategy in the United States and Japan indicates that while U.S. companies allocate more resources to short-term research and development, such as the implementation of existing products and manufacturing processes, Japanese companies spend more resources on long-term basic research or new product development.[3]

Care should be taken, therefore, to understand that even if the U.S. companies are in a better strategic budgeting position in regard to implementation of existing products and lines, they will be in a weaker position subsequently because of the failure to reposition research and development activity mixes among basic research, improvement of products, new product development, and improvement of manufacturing processes whenever changes make this necessary. Comparative data on both the ratio between the new products and new ventures and total sales over the past ten years, as well as the ratio between research and development costs and total sales, and the distribution of resource allocation to four research and development areas, are shown in Table 6.2

The same study provides comparative information on U.S. and Japanese companies in terms of five types of production technology: production by individual order, production by small lots, production by large lots, mass production, and system production, and non-routine use of production technologies. The basis of this taxonomy is considered in Table 6.3

The results indicate that while Japanese companies accept more non-routine types of production, such as individually ordered production and production in small lots, American companies accept more production in large lots. However, as far as mass production and equipment/device-oriented production are concerned, there are no significant differences. These findings may be attributed to the assumption that Japanese companies have been faced with more dynamic environments than American companies. They may also suggest that American companies need to be more adaptive and cost-effective in nonroutine production technology. This requirement should have bearing on the reexamination and repositioning of resources between production costing and process costing in the design and development of strategic budgeting.

In any case, one can hypothesize that successful strategic budgeting depends heavily upon identifying and implementing the share of research and development investment, one of the most important factors in long-term viability and growth of the corporation, compared with the share devoted to short-term resource allocation.

Ideally, the share allocated to technological breakthrough efforts should be continually and stably increased. In reality, however, because of excessively high interest rates and a prolonged recession, more and more companies rely heavily on short-term debt; and to get out from under the burden of short-term debt, which burdens their balance sheets by carrying $500 billion in debt, they reduce the basic research share.

Under such circumstances, maintaining the same level of research and development investment would be extremely difficult, even though the corporation realizes that research and development is a vital ingredient in coping with the international competition.

There are several ways to overcome the present "deadlocked" situation. First of all, the company should search for money at lower interest rates internationally. While average interest rates in the United States approached 20 percent in the first quarter of 1982, those in Japan at the same period were under 8 percent. Clearly, if money is available at such low rates, it should be borrowed to the fullest extent possible, in order to convert more expensive short-term debt into cheaper long-term debt, and thus strengthen the company.

TABLE 6.2. Comparative data on the ratio between new products and new ventures and total sales, and ratio between R&D costs and total sales over the past ten years, and the distribution of resource allotment for R&D areas.

Items	United States	Japan
Ratio between new products and new ventures and total sales in the past 10 years (%)	23.8 (23.9)	19.7 (22.6)
Ratio between R&D costs and total sales (%)	2.8 (2.91)	2.6 (2.66)
Distribution of resource allocation (%)		
Basic research*	8.4 (10.0)	15.9 (10.0)
Product improvement*	25.6 (19.4)	26.6 (18.3)
New product development†	29.9 (19.4)	33.9 (15.4)
Improvement of product process	36.1 (21.1)	23.6 (14.1)

Note: Numbers in parentheses indicate standard deviation.
* Significant at the level of 0.1%
† Significant at the level of 5%
Source: Tadao Kagano et al., "Strategy and Organization between U.S. and Japanese Companies," *Organizational Science* 15 (Summer 1981): 18.

TABLE 6.3. Comparative analysis of U.S. and Japanese types of production technologies.

Items	United States	Japan
Individually ordered production, such as made-to-order suits, custom devices (%)	12.5 (20.7)	20.2 (29.8)
Small-scale lot production, such as machine tools, dyestuffs, luxury women's apparel (%)	14.8 (19.9)	17.7 (25.1)
Large-scale lot production, such as parts, bottles, chemicals (%)	35.4 (32.7)	24.5 (32.8)
Mass production, such as automobiles, home electrical appliances (%)	19.3 (29.1)	22.6 (35.7)
System production, such as oil refining, synthetics (%)	17.9 (30.9)	15.0 (30.8)
Nonroutine technology	2.86 (0.95)	3.05 (1.12)

Note: Numbers in parentheses indicate standard deviations. The figures for nonroutine technology are derived by scoring the individually ordered production (5 points) to system production (7 points) and then by the ratio of the outputs of the corresponding firms.

Source: Tadao Kagano et al., "Strategy and Organization between U.S. and Japanese Companies," *Organizational Science* 15 (Summer 1981): 18.

126

In order to revitalize the world economy as well as the U.S. economy, the framework of a global financial structure is being assembled in Japan. According to this structure, a total of $500 billion will be collected and $25 billion will be invested annually to promote the effective use of excess production capacity and superior technology in the developed countries, in order to facilitate a smooth transfer of technology to the Third World countries, resolve the conflicts, and close the gaps between North and South, and East and West. This would represent a profitable use of excess OPEC funds.[4]

Second, an effective means of raising money to maintain and increase research and development investment is the issuance of zero-coupon bonds. Although the seller pays no interest during the 25- or 50-year life of the bond, he can deduct an imputed interest charge for tax purposes. However, since investors cannot deduct any part of the investment, the attraction of the bond depends upon the establishment of some sort of tax-exempt status for it.

Third, to stimulate equity investment for the generation of research and development funds, capital-gains taxes should be greatly reduced or eliminated. It appears that this is one of the quickest ways to replace old equity with new, and strengthen a company's competitive position.

Fourth, the long-awaited elimination of double taxation, under which both the corporation's earnings and dividends are taxed, should be facilitated, to ease the excessive tax burden on corporations.

Finally, but by no means least important, an economic planning and revitalization task force should be organized, to include representatives of the corporations, of Congress and the president's office, labor unions, and the Federal Reserve Bank to review the financial, taxation, and planning issues raised here on a long-term basis. Uncontrolled, arbitrary attempts to deal with them by legislation will only delay recovery from the present situation.

NOTES

1. *Business Week,* December 14, 1981, p. 52.
2. See, for example, Akira Ishikawa and Hiroshi Mieno, "Design and Evaluation of an Image Generator with Information Exchange," in G.E. Lasker, ed., *Applied Systems and Cybernetics* (New York: Pergamon Press, 1981), pp. 2341–45.
3. See, for more details, Tadao Kagano, Ikujiro Nonaka, Kiyonori Sakakibara, and Akihiro Okumura, "Strategy and Organization Between U.S. and Japanese Companies," *Organizational Science* 15, no. 2 (Summer 1981): 11–34. The comparative data for the U.S. and Japanese companies that are listed in the May and June 1979 issues of *Fortune* magazine as the top 100 in the mining and manufacturing industries, and 1,031 companies in manufacturing listed in the first and second parts of the Tokyo stock exchange were sought. The response from the United States was 227 companies (22.7 percent), including General Motors, duPont, Mobil, and Ford, compared with 291 companies in Japan, including Hitachi, Matsuhita, Mitsubishi, Fujitsu, and Toyo Rayon.
4. *Yomiuri Shimbun* (Daily Yomiuri News), January 1, 1982, p. 1.

Case Studies of Strategic Budgeting

——7——

Now it is time to review various cases of strategic budgeting, to see how fundamentals and principles of strategic budgeting have been applied, the manner in which strategic planning is linked with budgetary control, what innovative forces or creative efforts are involved in these cases, and what concepts and techniques are applied in each case.

First, we shall look at the case of ABC International, already partially discussed. This is a real case, although names of the companies, figures, and formats have been disguised. The main theme of this case is the evolution of the relationship of short-term budgeting to strategic budgeting. The reader will see the creative formats developed for strategic analysis and, eventually, the linkage to budgeting actions.

The second case is that of the Canon Company, well-known for cameras, lenses, and copying machines, headquartered in Japan. Emphasis here will be on Canon's long-term or strategic planning simulation system, so that the linkage of strategic planning to budgeting will be clearly revealed. (This simulation model is adopted from *Cases of the Most Recent Strategic Planning,* by Professor Toyohiro Kohno of Gakushuin University, Tokyo: Dobunkan, 1978, pp. 147–172.)

Finally, the case of Apollo Industries will be discussed. This case highlights the application of one of the strategic planning techniques, profit impact of marketing strategy (PIMS). Here, the focus will be on the way in which strategic analyses can be made, rather than on the linkage between strategic planning and budgetary control. Note, however, that a successful strategic analysis can, in most cases, provide ready access to budgeting by identifying key assumptions and figures that are the starting points of budgeting.

CASE 1: TRUCK-LIGHT, A DIVISION OF BETA CORPORATION, AN ABC INTERNATIONAL COMPANY

Evolution of Planning Cycle from One-Year Budgeting to Strategic Budgeting

Truck-Light is a division of Beta Corporation, which in turn is a subsidiary of ABC International. It manufactures truck lighting equipment, emergency vehicle lighting and sirens, truck mirrors, reflectors, truck air-conditioning components, and tire gauges. It is considered by many to be a leader in the truck lighting industry.

Because Truck-Light is not an independent entity and must function in accordance with both Beta Corporation and ABC International regulatory constraints, it reflects these constraints in both management policies and budgeting practices. Truck-Light must comply with all corporate directives and must maintain uniform reporting formats in order to allow uniform consolidation of earnings and other financial data.

The accounting structure consists of a vice president/comptroller, an assistant comptroller, a cost accounting manager, a budget manager, a payroll supervisor, a receivables manager, and an accounts payable supervisor. There is also a full staff of accountants and clerical personnel.

The reader will recognize that the Japanese approach is highly logico-mathematical, while the American approach is less mathematical (in terms of the application of basic algebra only) and attempts to embrace more alternatives, recognizing uncertainties.

Note, however, that even logico-mathematical approaches need to incorporate various kinds of policy variables into the models and simulation systems. Thus, the essential point is whether those inputs are realistic and feasible.

Again, the author cannot help stressing the importance and significance of an insightful reading, judgment, and belief on the part of both those who provide input (those who decide the number of a decision variable and those who identify the basic and unique alternatives of scenarios, if descriptive approaches are to be taken) and decision makers.

The very long-range approach, as shown in Chapter 3, the contingency approach in Chapter 4, the cross-impact approach in Chapter 5 and the comparison of U.S. and Japanese research and development in Chapter 6 will help in developing such insightful concepts and numbers, but above all, strategic budgeting concepts and approaches should be a solid basis for creative and feedforward endeavors.

The budgeting and planning process at Truck-Light was relatively unchanged prior to the 1980 budget (business plan). It consisted of the following:

1. Commentary

2. Budget package—profit/loss statement, one-year
                       balance sheet, one-year
                       profit/loss, five-year projection

3. Facilities plan—capital spending, one-year.

The business-plan cycle normally begins with the analysis of current-year and prior-year sales/profit by product line. This consists of a detailed listing of product sales and standard margin (standard cost system) for several years and the latest year's activity. After these data are prepared by the budget manager, they are presented to the vice-presidents of marketing and sales. After the sales personnel review the data, a meeting of the president of the company, the vice-presidents of sales and marketing, the vice-president/comptroller, and the budget manager is scheduled to discuss significant sales trends, company goals, and industry statistics.

New product requirements are also discussed at this meeting, in order to determine capital requirements. After all the issues are resolved, the sales department is normally required to complete the sales projection for each product, along with sales curve data and price increase projections. It should be noted that sales and marketing offer similar products, but with drastically different pricing structures, so that adjustments are required in order to maintain consistent pricing structures.

Upon completion of these schedules, which require a broad knowledge of the industry, a total sales projection in sales dollars and units is submitted to the president for review and approval. If it meets general expectations and growth projections, it receives preliminary approval and is then distributed to the cost department for a detailed analysis of the standard cost of each item and the intended cost increases. The manufacturing department must also review the sales projections in order to establish capacity requirements and manning forecasts.

During the three- or four-month period in which data are compiled, specific instructions and schedules needed by the corporate offices are received around May, and additional requests for data are distributed. At the same time the sales forecasts are being distributed, cost-of-capacity budget schedules are submitted to the individual department supervisors and managers. These schedules require a detailed listing of all personnel, salary information and proposed spending for travel and entertainment, office supplies, contributions, dues, and employee benefits. These must be reviewed and approved by the vice-presidents of manufacturing, sales, administration, or research and development, depending on the area of responsibility. After all data on sales, standard costs, personnel, manufacturing levels, and other items are obtained and compiled (normally around June), a preliminary profit/loss statement and balance sheet are presented to the president and the comptroller. A meeting is then scheduled and changes are recommended or implemented.

After a final draft is agreed upon, all assumptions and commentary are assembled along with corporate reporting forms. This preliminary package is then sent to the group head, who has responsibility for five to six divisions, for review. The president of Truck-Light presents his budget to the group head in New York, and further revisions are often required. In many instances three or four meetings with the group head are required before the final budget can be prepared. In past years, drastic reductions have been needed in capital appropriations because of the high interest rates and cost of capital. Additional reductions in invested capital (inventory, receivables, cash) have also been mandated because of the emphasis on return on invested capital rather than return on sales.

This new emphasis on balance sheet items rather than on the conventional profit/loss statement resulted in a strategic approach to the budgeting cycle. This drastic move away from the normal budget approach forced management to analyze present return on invested capital and to review methods of improving it. The first step was to have each unit obtain industry statistics, sales volumes, and data on competitors. The industry association's credit agency data and personal interviews with sales personnel familiar with the industry were used to obtain financial and managerial data on competitors. Competitors were then ranked on planning assumption schedules, so that a better perspective regarding market share and company strengths and weaknesses could be obtained. After all these data were compiled, meetings were held to establish goals on market penetration and improvements in return on investment.

In an effort to promote company growth, a series of "jump out" decisions was requested by corporate headquarters. This enabled management to submit radical proposals, such as plant consolidations, product line discontinuations, and major capital expenditures (and their effects on future growth and return on invested capital). If these options were approved by corporate headquarters, they were inserted into the preliminary budgets. In the case of Truck-Light, a plant consolidation was proposed but was not inserted into either the one-year budget or the strategic five-year forecast.

This new approach to planning enables management to suggest other areas of investment to maximize return on investment. It was accepted by all levels of management in Truck-Light. It also provided much-needed industry data.

Formats for the Truck-Light Strategic Plan

The following section demonstrates the format used in the Truck-Light strategic plan:

1. Market size
2. Market share
3. Competitive margin, 1985
4. Market margin
5. Key success factors, 1985.

FIGURE 7.1.   ABC International strategic planning assumptions: Analysis of market size.

The major product lines manufactured by Truck-Light are lighting devices, switches, mirrors and emergency flashing lights for the truck, trailer and bus vehicle markets. Tire hardware including tire valves, gauges, air hose fittings and nozzles are made by the Acme Tire Facility.

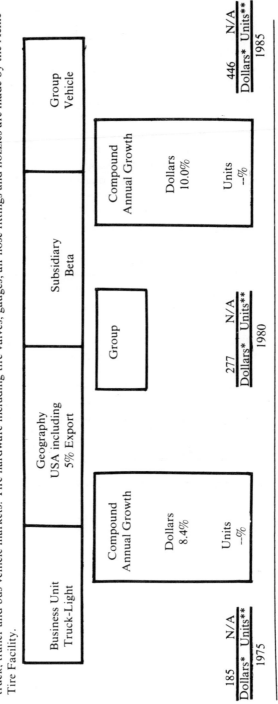

*Use nominal dollars for 1975 and 1980. Use 1985 dollars with inflation assumptions from long-range plans for 1984; specify inflation rate used.

**Please specify the units (cases, ounces, tons, units, etc.) if applicable.

Major Causes of Change	Explanation of Past Development	Rationale for Current Situation	Assumptions for the Future
Customer, such as: - Demographic trends - Number of potential customers - Lifestyle trends	Revenue ton miles continue to increase. Industry continued to expand to the South and West.	Continued trend toward trucks serving smaller communities versus rail service.	80% of our business is to short haul truckers. Economics continue to favor LCL truck shipments versus rail. End users will continue to require prompt delivery.
Competitive action, such as: - Imports/exports - Competitor entries/exits - New technology/new products - Overcapacity		Alpha, Gamma and Truck-Light all responding to customer demand for long-life bulb products. No clearly established market leader.	
Government action, such as: - Taxes - Duties - Regulation - Legislation	Strict government regulations established a barrier to new competitors as well as stimulated mandated demand for our products.		

Source: Prepared by author.

FIGURE 7.2. ABC International strategic planning assumptions: Analysis of competitive margin.

Major Areas of Cost Differences	Explanation of Past Development	Rationale for Current Situation	Assumptions for the Future
Product Costs - Fixed - Variable	Truck-Light's weakness in engineering and manufacturing resulted in higher product costs.	$2.8 million write-off at Truck-Light due to balance sheet adjustment.	Truck-Light will lower costs substantially be intense cost reduction efforts.
Distribution	Delta's location in Syracuse, New Yorkk, increased their distribution costs.	Truck-Light's after—market freight costs are low because of large markets in Northeast close to shipping warehouse.	
R&D/Engineering	Truck-Light's low investment in engineering and research and evelopment was far below Gamma and Delta.	Truck-Light engineering and manufacturing engineering staff inadequate, resulting in high product cost.	Professional engineering and manufacturing staff will be employed at Truck-Light.
Advertising and promotion		Sales Promotions were poorly controlled and not professionally planned.	Wasteful sales promotions discontinued.
Selling Costs	Truck-light's low selling costs are due primarily to large OEM Detroit sales.		Truck-Light selling costs reduced by better territory alignment and better controls on expenses.
Other Costs	Other (3.0) result of sale of Truck-Light flasher division.		

Source: Prepared by author.

FIGURE 7.3. ABC International strategic planning assumptions: Analysis of market margin.

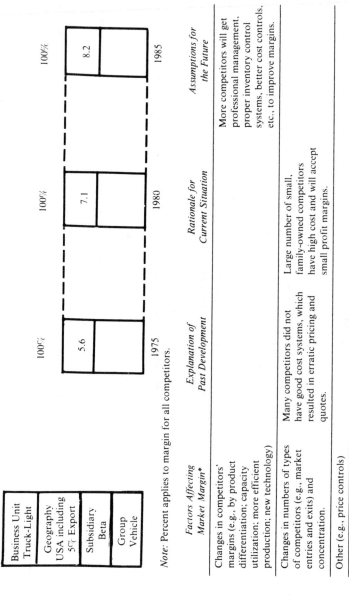

Business Unit Truck-Light

Geography USA including 5% Export

Subsidiary Beta

Group Vehicle

100%	100%	100%
5.6	7.1	8.2
1975	1980	1985

Note: Percent applies to margin for all competitors.

Factors Affecting Market Margin*	Explanation of Past Development	Rationale for Current Situation	Assumptions for the Future
Changes in competitors' margins (e.g., by product differentiation; capacity utilization; more efficient production; new technology)			More competitors will get professional management. proper inventory control systems, better cost controls. etc., to improve margins.
Changes in numbers of types of competitors (e.g., market entries and exits) and concentration.	Many competitors did not have good cost systems, which resulted in erratic pricing and quotes.	Large number of small, family-owned competitors have high cost and will accept small profit margins.	
Other (e.g., price controls)			

*"Margin" defined as the percentage of revenue available after costs identified in Figure 7.2.
Source: Prepared by author.

TABLE 7.1. ABC International strategic planning assumptions: Analysis of market share

Major Causes of Change	Explanation of Past Development	Rationale for Current Situation	Assumptions for the Future
Environmental, such as energy Other	Sales demand is cyclical. Period experienced moderate real growth. Price inflation averaged 5.7%		Includes 8% price inflation per year
Source of absolute numbers	Historical data	Personal knowledge	
Products (including changes in price, technology)	Truck-Light's market share varied widely by product line. High market share in lamps offset by low market share in mirrors	Prior Truck-Light management emphasized sales growth. Approximately 13% of sales were marginally profitable	Truck-Light will increase market share in truck mirrors by becoming more competitive by lowering costs. Also, NHTSA will require more mirrors per truck
Costs (including changes in process, sources, production technology)	Gamma, Equipment, Pate had substantially lower manufacturing costs, and best engineering and manufacturing	Truck-Light was a high-cost producer and generally sold at 10% higher prices in after-market	Truck-Light now purchases 50% of mirror products; more efficient production will reverse this trend
Sales/service (including changes in sales forces, major accounts, distribution sytem)		Truck-Light has dominant position in after-market distribution, which is Gamma's weakness	
Other	Delta had very few new products 1974-79. K-D, Do-Ray Pathfinder, and Yankee all had minimal profits	Delta hurt by internal disputes. Equipment recently gained market share when Delta Dominion began distribution of its long-life products	Major cost reductions from plant consolidation will result in greater market penetration by Truck-Light

Source: Prepared by author.

FIGURE 7.4. ABC International strategic planning assumptions: Key success factors, 1985.

Business Unit Truck-Light	Subsidiary Beta
Geography USA including 5% Export	Group Vehicle

Competitive Positioning:

X = ABCI Unit
m = Delta
• = Gamma

Key Success Factors*	Importance Rank	Low	Medium	High	Options/Opportunities for the Future
- Innovative technology	2	m		X •	Professional engineering department can provide redesigned and newly designed products to improve market position.
P					
R					
O - Engineering services	2		X	m	
D - Clear branded differentiation					
U					
C - Other product factors					
T					

138

- Manufacturing engineering	2			X		Newly established manufacturing engineering department can contribute to substantial cost reductions by means of new processes, methods, and standards.
C						
O - Production technology						
S - Operations management	3	m	•	X		
T - Other cost factors — plant consolidation	2	m			X	Preliminary study indicates cost savings in excess of $1 million per year. Indications are Delta will remain in Syracuse, New York.

S - Sales force					
E - Distribution system	1		•	m	X
A **R**					
L **V** - Location of facilities					
E **I**					
S **C** - Other sales/service factors					
E					

* This list is illustrative; adjust/add as necessary. Complete the positioning *only* for those factors you feel are truly important.

Source: Prepared by author.

139

TABLE 7.2. Estimated 1980 sales. Truck-Light and competitors (million dollars).

	Pretax Margin* (%)	Total Sales	Pretax Margin* ($)	Comments
Truck-Light	--	$44.1	--	Includes 1.4 Gamma Cab and 5.4 Alpha
Gamma	12.0	25.03.0		
Delta	6.0	29.0	1.74	Includes 9.0 NAPA
Pate	10..5	15.6	1.64	
Equipment	11.0	12.0	1.32	Division of Quaker State
Yankee	2.0	13.2	.26	
K-D Lamp	4.0	11.0	.44	
Pathfinder	5.0	14.0	.70	Division of Allen Group
Arrow Safety Device	5.0	5.4	.27	
Federal Sign and Signal	10.0	12.0	1.20	
Whelan	10.0	9.0	.90	
Delbar Products	9.0	25.0	2.25	company produces mirrors only
Velvac	8.0	10.0	.80	
Dominion	12.0	29.0	3.48	4.0 are U.S. sales and 25.0 Canadian sales
Weldon, Inc.	7.0	2.1	.15	
Do-Ray Lamp	2.0	4.6	.09	
Roberk	9.0	9.0	.81	Division of Parker-Hannifin
	7.1*	$270.0	19.05	

*Average of four selected competitors, excluding interest and depreciation.
Note: Other competition (not listed) had approximately $7.0 million in sales.

Management was allowed to select various methods of increasing market penetration. This entailed the following:

1. Explanation of "option"
2. "Reach out" vs. "leap out" decision
3. "Leap out" vs. base case (no change)
4. Profit/loss effects of "reach out"
5. Capital ROI.

Option:

Expand geographic territory through acquisition of Canadian company and a Mexican partner.

After two very costly false starts, Truck-Light currently does virtually no business in Canada. The Canadian market is approximately $31 million, with Dominion Auto having $24 million, Do Ray Canada $4.5 million, and Gamma Manufacturing $2.5 million. Dominion has dominated the market because of protective tariffs. Gamma attempted to attack this market through distribution only, with no manufacturing facilities, and after seven years still has not realized any profits. Do Ray Canada, on the other hand, was originally started by Do Ray-United States, and later taken over and managed by two Canadians, Jules and Murray Poizner. They have successfully turned this company around; it is now growing and profitable. On 1979 sales of $3.9 million, they had pretax profits of $392,000.

A decision has been made to enter into a buy-sell agreement with Do Ray whereby it will market Truck-Light's product line throughout Canada. It has a wholly owned subsidiary, Newark Tool and Machine, a metal stamping facility combined with a tool and die operation, that is directed by Jules Poizner, one of the owners.

Do Ray appears to be the only firm in Canada positioned to make a serious penetration of that market and Dominion's monopoly. Its operation, combined with Truck-Light, should give all of the tools necessary to become a strong force in the Canadian marketplace.

Investments would be minimal, since Do Ray Canada would be purchasing Truck-Light products and the latter's only investments at this time would be for tooling. It is important to note that the laws relating to vehicle lighting in Canada are identical to those in the United States even though the penalties are somewhat different. Therefore the market growth should be assured. Figures 7.5–7.8 show strategic option worksheets used in reaching the decision.

Mexico, on the other hand, has no legal requirements for truck lighting and has only half the vehicles of Canada: 4.5 million versus 9 million. The lack of legal requirements diminishes this market even though the entire Mexican economy will be growing at a very strong rate for the next five to ten years. Truck-Light should participate in the Mexican market through the sale of its products to a firm named Optiro, which manufactures and distributes automotive and other products throughout Mexico. Two thirds of this firm are owned by Hella, a large German automotive parts manufacturer. Truck-Light has just begun to participate in this market through the sale of its products to Optiro and believes this market can be improved to approximately $500,000 per year within the next two to three years. It is also possible that Truck-Light can import products from Optiro, utilizing the latter's low-cost labor for some of its labor-intensive, low-cost product needs. Truck-Light will look further at the Mexican market in the next few months; the examination will culminate in a visit to the Optiro plant on August 19 and 20, at which time there will be a discussion with the principals on the future of their company and their possible desire to have a U.S. partner. This company has 1,200 employees and is a large supplier to Volkswagen. While the market appears quite limited at the present time, there should be a full investigation of the opportunities, in view of the predicted rapid growth of the Mexican economy.

CASE 2: CANON, INC.

Strategic Budgeting with Planning Simulation System

Canon, Incorporated, has been known as a designer, developer, manufacturer, and marketer of high-technology, high-quality products since its founding in 1937 in Japan. Its main lines are cameras—it is proud of being the world's largest manufacturer of 35mm single-lens reflex models; business machines, including plain paper copiers, calculators, and other equipment; and industrial and medical optical equipment. The company markets its products under the Canon name in more than 130 countries. Direct employees in all areas numbered more than 20,000 as of December 31, 1980.

The internal organizaton is a matrix structure in which the three product groups are horizontal profit centers (see Figure 7.9). They are photo products, business machines, and optical products. Vertical links are provided by R&D, manufacturing, and marketing committees, with geographic marketing subsidiaries.

The Canon annual report for 1980, written by Dr. Hajime Mitarai, contains the following statements:

> Our growth depends greatly on technological innovation. Our best-selling products—the AE-1 camera, NP-200 copier, and PLA-500FA mask aligner, among others—all started in Canon laboratories.
>
> When we began in 1937, Japan's technological level was just high enough to build bicycles. We wanted to make Cadillacs.
>
> Now we have become Japan's first 35mm focal-plane shutter camera manufacturer. Japan leads the world in 35mm single-lens reflex cameras, and Canon leads the industry.

FIGURE 7.5. ABC International Strategic Option Worksheet: Option I, Sheet 1.

Business Unit Truck-Light	Subsidiary Beta		Geography North America			Group Vehicle		ABCI Unit Relative Position

	Market Size	X	Market Margin	=	Market Attractiveness	X	Relative Share	X	Relative Margin	=	

Base Case: $446.0 × 8.2% = $36.6 × 1.40 × 1.659 = 2.323

ABCI Unit Share .140 ÷ Largest Competitive Share .100

ABCI Unit Margin .136 + Market Margin .082

Option Economics: X = =

ABCI Unit Share .140 ÷ Largest Competitive Share .100

ABCI Unit Margin .136 + Market Margin .082

Revised Unit Economics: $446.0 × 8.2% = $36.6 × 1.51 × 1.646 = 2.485

ABCI Unit Share .151 ÷ Largest Competitive Share .10

ABCI Unit Margin .135 + Market Margin .082

Source: Prepared by author.

FIGURE 7.6. ABC International strategic option worksheet: Option I, Sheet 2.

Business Unit Truck-Light	Subsidiary Beta
Geography North America	Group Vehicle

Date Case	Reach Out	Leap Out
☐	☒	☐

(Check One)

Option summary description. Expand geographic market through acquisition of Canadian company and a Mexican partner.

144

Issues	Subissues	Analysis
1. How attractive are the Mexican/ Canadian markets		- Market size and five-year growth - Market margins - Market leader and share
2. What criteria are to be used in evaluating acquisition candidates	- Distribution capability - Manufacturing capability - Management quality - Financial performance - Market standing, including share and product line coverage - Investment requirements	- Develop and rank criteria evaluating attractiveness of acquisition candidates
3. Who are the attractive acquisition candidates		- Identify and evaluate the leading acquisition candidate in each market
4. Identify our relative competitive position with each acquisition		- Estimate our share and relative margin in each market over the next five years

Source: Prepared by author.

145

FIGURE 7.7. ABC International strategic option worksheet: Option I, Sheet 3.

Business Unit Truck-Light
Geography North America
Subsidiary Beta
Group Vehicle

Option summary description:
Expand geographic market through Canadian expansion.

Date Case ☐   Reach Out ☒   Leap Out ☐

(Check One)

Risk assessment: Low risk, as products will be similar or same as those already marketed.

Factor	Base Case	Revised Unit Economics	Rationale/Explanation
Market size	446.0	446.0	Market size does not change from base case since Canadian market was included.
Market margin	8.2	8.2	Market size does not change from base case since Canadian market was included.
Market attractiveness	36.6	36.6	Market size does not change from base case since Canadian market was included.

Relative share	1.40	1.51	Truck-Light market share increase $5 million by 1985 with $3 million due to Canadian market penetration and $2 million due to sale of new Canadian products (buy outs) in United States.
Relative margin	1.659	1.646	This shows a slight decrease due to the incremental sales achievement at 12% margin versus overall base margin of 13.6%.
Competitive position	2.323	2.485	Increase due to market penetration increase to $5 million.
Financial:			For the five-year period ending 1985 tooling investment will be $210,000. In year 1985, additional capital requirements for inventory and working capital will be $833,333 and $450,000, respectively.
Skills:	Already available.		
Staff:	Will be marketed through Do-Ray (Canada), Ltd. organization, which is already in place.		
Timing:	Expect to enter market third quarter 1980.		

Source: Prepared by author.

FIGURE 7.8. ABC International Strategic Option Worksheet: Option I, Sheet 4.

| Business Unit Truck-Light |
| Geography North America |
| Subsidiary Beta |
| Group Vehicle |

	Date Case	Reach Out	Leap Out
	☐	☒	☐

Option summary description:
Expand geographic market through Canadian expansion.

	1981	1982	1983	1984	1985
Sales ($)	$150,000	$1,500,000	$2,500,000	$3,700,000	$5,000,000
Pretax earnings*($)	15,000	180,000	300,000	444,000	600,000

Pretax margin (%)	10.0	12.0	12.0	12.0	12.0
Investment required ($)					
- By year	$123,500	376,500	296,667	358,000	393,666
- Cumulative	68,500	445,000	741,667	1,099,667	1,493,333
ROIC** (%)	21,9	40.4	40.4	40.4	40.2

* Pretax earnings do not include depreciation, fixed charges (corporate overhead charges/fees), interest charges.
** Pretax earnings ÷ cumulative investment.

Capital	$30,000	$ 60,000	$100,000	$150,000	$210,000
Inventory	25,000	250,000	416,667	616,667	833,333
Net	68,500	135,000	225,000	333,000	450,000
	$123,500	$445,000	$741,667	$1,099,667	$1,493,333

Source: Prepared by author.

149

FIGURE 7.9.   Matrix structure of Canon, Inc.

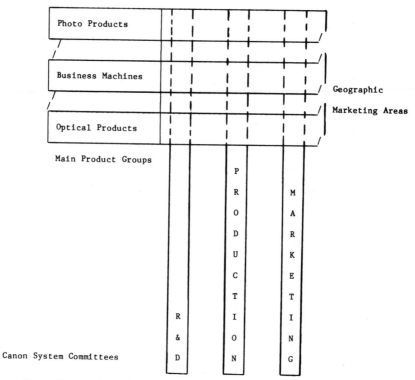

Source: Prepared by author.

About 1,300 engineers and scientists work in our research and development laboratories, representing 15 percent of the parent company's work force. The distribution of their specialties is unusually well-balanced: mechanical engineering and electronics; physics (including optics) and chemistry; and sophisticated computer software.

These capabilities enable us to apply precisely the right combination of technologies to any development project. Our research system is open-minded and offers attractive opportunities to researchers. It's designed to encourage innovation, not to hamstring scientists with bureaucratic rules. As a result Canon appeals to bright young researchers, both new university graduates and engineers who join us from other firms.

Canon's R&D organization is divided into two sections: product research and corporate research. Product research is aimed at new products to be marketed in a two- to three-year span. Corporate research is longer-term and includes more speculative projects.

Patents are one concrete measure of research output; Canon's engineers have 10,500 patent applications to their credit since 1971. We lead the camera and business machine industries in patents, both in Japan and among Japanese companies in America. We also sell more technology than we buy, by a ratio of 5:1.

Canon's R&D objectives are high added value and top quality in products and efficiency in getting ideas to market.... In 1978 we began a program to cut average product development time in half, from drawing board to marketplace, with the use of computer-aided design and manufacturing. The key to shortening development time is an unchanging goal for each project.

Take the Canonword 55 Japanese word processor, for example. Japanese is written with thousands of complex ideographs as well as two phonetic syllabaries. As a result, Japanese keyboards are so cumbersome that even the most skillful operators average only 40 characters per minute. Our objective was a word processor as easy to use as an English typewriter.

The answer in this case was to enter the characters phonetically and then tap the machine's memory bank to find the character itself. Canon developed the Canonword 55 in less than three years, including concept development.

It is like the bicyble and the Cadillac. With word processors, and in any other field we tackle, we'll meet the challenges we set for ourselves.

The progress Canon has made to date can be visualized as tending in two directions: internationalism and diversification.

The mental basis of its business activities also developed as internationalization and diversification, and the attitude of employees can be summarized by two following management doctrines: to contribute to the rise in culture by making the best product in the world, and to attain continuous prosperity by establishing an ideal company.

In other words, by producing unique, reliable, excellent products and by contributing to the improvement of the lives and cultures of the people of the world, Canon's workers believe they will be able to improve themselves, and thus be able to develop an ideal company that can bring about lasting prosperity and an enriched life.

The style of the company may be represented as performance-oriented, healthism (health first), new familism, and three selfs actualization. Performance orientation is a move to get rid of scholastic-records-oriented thinking, or evaluating on the basis of the name or reputation of the university from which one has graduated. By so doing, Canon feels it can identify the most qualified person and locate him or her in the best place. To achieve this realistically, the professional ability qualification system was established, and it is available to every employee.

Healthism grew out of the idea that all fundamentals in the company, as well as in the individual's life, begin with the maintenance of health. Taking into consideration fair competition with its Western counterparts, Canon established the first 40-hour work week in Japan.

New familism is the belief that the company will prosper through all working together with reciprocal understanding and mutual trust. This is different from the old familism, in which there was a powerful boss and the rest of the members were treated as subordinates.

Finally, three selfs-actualization means self-motivation, self-activation, and self-control, the factors that will enable each employee to improve his or her capabilities and develop to the fullest extent.

Planning and Budgeting System

Canon's planning and budgeting system consists of three components:

1. Strategic planning and budgeting system (SPB)
2. Intermediate planning and budgeting system (IPB)
3. Short-range planning and budgeting system (APB).

The core of the SPB is to establish the direction and goal, then control the transition, of the corporate environment in order to achieve qualitative innovation in all areas of the corporate structure.

AFB is a program action plan that is fully quantified and corresponds directly to the duties and responsibilities of each segment of the organization within a given budget operating period.

Let us look more closely into the strategic aspect of SPB in Canon, Inc. This history of strategic (or long-range) planning begins with the first endeavor in 1962–67.

The Doubling Plan for Individual Salaries, established by Prime Minister Ikeda and his cabinet in 1960, supplied the impetus for long-range planning. At that time 95 percent of Canon's sales were cameras, but there was a feeling that the firm could not rely solely on these sales because cameras were reaching the saturation point in the product cycle. Canon needed other lines to achieve substantial growth.

Accordingly, since it already had the technologies of optics and the precision machinery, in the first long-range planning period Canon started to establish a diversification plan, mainly in the area of clerical machinery and equipment. By the last year of the First Long-Range Plan (1966), it was planned to reduce camera sales to 20 percent of total sales.

The Second Long-Range Plan covered 1968–72. Its objectives were the following:

1. To realize the diversification required by the First Long-Range Plan.
2. To enlarge production capacity to meet requirements of increased demand.
3. To establish an export system so that Canon products could be sold all over the world under their own brand names.

During this period, product lines broke out of the mold of the camera industry to a new industry that included cameras. In this new industry, internationalization and diversification were developed continuously.

In 1971, with the collapse of the gold monetary standard, the world entered an era of confusion. Bearing in mind the arrival of a new order of world economy, Canon had to plan how it would achieve stable growth in this turbulent environment. The outcome was the Third Long-Range Plan (1973–77). While the first two plans were somewhat extrapolative and quantitative, the Third Plan is considered to be more qualitative. Its main theme is expressed in six goals:

1. Building the foundation of a new corporate structure
2. Changing to a quality-oriented enterprise
3. Moving into the reflex information market
4. Moving toward a more intelligence-oriented company
5. Increasing the effectiveness of the whole Canon group
6. Building the foundation of an international company.

During the Third Plan period, sales increased 210 percent, exports reached 70 percent, and the rate of sales excluding cameras reached 44 percent, evidence of the achievement of established goals.

The Fourth Long-Range Plan (1978–83) is aimed at establishing a firm foundation in the reflex information industry, preempting the anticipated transitions and adapting to the uncertain environment. The ultimate objective in this period is to become one of the leading international firms in the area of image information.

Canon's Strategic Planning Simulation System

While the objective of the First, Second and Third Long-Range Plans shifted emphasis to quality from quantity, the goals and framework of these plans have been quantity-oriented. After the Third Long-Range Plan, the management simulation model (CLPS) previously developed started to be utilized.

Development of this model began in 1969. At first it was not developed along product lines, and involved 2,000 program steps. The concept of the enterprise by products, adopted in 1970, encompassed headquarters and several divisions instead of the entire company. With this revision, the program steps numbered 3,500. Further implementation and revision incorporated the idea of integration and aggregation, and additional functions into the model.

Objectives of this simulation model are the following:

1. Speed up computations
2. More accurate results
3. Discovery of the problem areas of strategic planning
4. Access to profit and loss by product groups.

The discovery of problem areas can be done by outputting ten-period (on a quarterly or yearly basis) profit-and-loss statements, balance sheets, labor cost planning sheets, and capital investment planning sheets. Problem areas can be discovered at the earliest possible time by changing the values of policy variables.

There are four characteristics of the simulation model. First, it is macroscopic. This means the relationships are omitted below the level of product groups. It does, however, maintain the basic units of product groups, such as cameras, calculators, and copying machines; and they are captured in yen and gross.

Second, it makes possible a long-term forecast over ten years should yearly data be input. The same is the case with a five-year forecast if semiannual data are adopted.

Third, it can accommodate up to ten product groups—for instance nine groups and one headquarters.

Fourth, it is a computer-based simulation model.

The units of computation and output are by product groups because, first, there are substantial differences in the methods of production and marketing of the product groups. Therefore, without identifying the corresponding parameters and policy variables, no effective analysis could be made. Second, judgment regarding future product mixes is essential for strategic planning, and the simulation should be of assistance in such policy decisions.

Planning by product groups is built by means of seven programs.

In the sales program, the initial computation is done by inputting the ten estimates made on the basis of corporate policies. The sales estimate itself cannot be made with this model, but by use of other submodels. All numbers are based on either dollars or yen, and prices are based upon the number of units sold.

In the production program, upon determining the sales estimates, the required production can be determined automatically, taking into consideration the inventories available. Inventory increases or decreases are computed on the turnover period. Whether increasing or decreasing, inventory is a policy variable and is subject to the kinds of production groups. The numbers are also denoted in terms of currency (yen).

In the personnel and labor cost program, the personnel program is split into manufacturing and nonmanufacturing. Personnel estimates in the manufacturing area are based on the amount of production per employee. This amount is assumed to increase year by year, and is fixed by the following formulas:

Amount of production at $(t-1)(1+$efficiency increase rate$)=$amount of production at t.

Total production/amount of production at t=required number of personnel at t.

In R&D, general administration, and sales, the required number of personnel is directly input.

Personnel costs consist of basic pay, severance pay, overtime pay, bonuses, and welfare and incentive pay. All are input as policy variables.

In the pro forma statement program, computations are basically made following the order of preparing financial statements. Operating and nonoperating income are computed by product groups. Taxes, dividends, and retained earnings are computed independently, in order to determine the economics and profitability of each product group.

This is the practice in the construction of balance sheets. Evaluation is made to see if each group is profitable, just as if it were a different company.

In the management indices program, since pro forma financial statements cannot fully uncover how the goals are being attained and where gaps exist, four categories of indices are constructed: growth, profitability, stability, and social responsibility. A list of indices is then made.

In the functional program, programs related to R&D and general administration are defined as functional. In these areas, attention is concentrated on cost only, since neither production nor sales are involved. The basic approach is quite similar to the one adopted for the manufacturing area.

In the corporate program, programs from both manufacturing and nonmanufacturing are integrated. The following are representative outputs:

1. An overall personnel program
2. An overall investment program
3. Profit-and-loss statement and profit distribution program
4. Balance sheet
5. A list of management indices.

Future issues related to this simulation are listed below.

1. In this simulation, sales are split into domestic and foreign sales by product groups, and given as the value of externally determined policy. No automatic computation is made. The reason is that the change of these product markets is very fast, and the rate of export is 70 percent, both of which make it very difficult to extrapolate.

   Therefore, markets where the existing methods are available are predicted by using the techniques of demand forecast, while others are forecast by comparing the above results with the cumulative numbers and adding educated guesses and intuitive feelings.
2. In an industry such as Canon, the power of production is represented by the capacity of workers. Therefore, the capital investment program is built by "the equipped rate to the workers." Canon believes this concept will be valid from now on because it is aiming at the leading position in the sophisticated assembly industry, R&D industry, and intelligence-intensive industry.
3. This model does not incorporate automatic feedback processes, whereby the gap between expected goals and actual output is automatically adjusted. In other words, one-time input brings about one-time output. The frequency of repeating this, along with the parallel development of more artificial-intelligence-oriented models, would overcome this weakness to a great extent.
4. Finally, this model is intended to use financial data, crude or processed, as directly as possible. However, since the prepared financial data contain more meaningful information, the result would be much better. A list of representative outputs is shown in Table 7.3.

TABLE 7.3. Canon's simulation model.

Strategic (Long-Term Planning and Budgeting)	Medium-Term P&B	Short-Term P&B
Planning and Budgeting System		
Corporate policy and strategic development	Strategic deployment program by divisions	Execution of annual programs
Time horizon implementation and revision		
5 years	3 years	1 year
Relatively fixed	Revised annually	
Aims		
Deciding the direction to follow	Guiding P&B from medium-term perspectives	Short-range profit program
Qualitative innovation	Proceeding to strategic project	Budgetary control stressed
Motivating employees	Optimum allocation of resources	
Variables	*Distinction*	*Instruction*
Sales Program		
Total sales (domestic)	Given externally	Another model is used
Market share	Policy variable	Decided in advance

156

Framework of Subsystems and Programs

Program by Product Groups	Functional Program	Corporate Integrated Program
Sales program (domestic)		
Adjusted sales	Computed	Multiplication of the above
Amount of exports	Given externally	Cumulated by regions
Market share	Policy variable	Decided by regions
Adjusted export	Computed	Multiplication of the above
Total sales (domestic and foreign)	Computed	The sum of adjusted sales
Production program		
Personnel and labor costs	Personnel costs	Total personnel and labor costs
Investment program	Investment	Integrated investment program
Cost of goods sold	Other expenses	
P&L statement and profit distribution program		Integrated P&L and profit distribution program
Balance sheet		Integrated balance sheet
Management control indices		Corporate management control indices

Source: Prepared by author.

CASE 3: APOLLO INDUSTRIES

Apollo's Goals and Objectives

Apollo Industries, a large, publicly held, broadly diversified corporation, has chosen the corporate goal of maximizing stockholder wealth, as measured by the market price of its common stock. Top management believes this can best be accomplished through the objective of maximizing the present value of net cash flow for each business in its portfolio.

The PIMS proxy for this measurement of financial performance is DCF+R: discounted cash flow for ten years plus the present value of the business's residual value of fixed assets. Apollo's management has therefore elected to pursue a strategy which optimizes DCF+R for each business in its portfolio.

Apollo's management has a second objective. This pertains to cash balance among the businesses in its portfolio. After generating cash sufficient to pay a current dividend to stockholders, the cash-using businesses in the portfolio should need approximately the amount of cash provided by the cash-generating businesses in the portfolio. This objective minimizes the necessity of procuring external financing in the capital markets. Accordingly, Apollo desires that some businesses in its portfolio be such that DCF+R is optimized by growing market share and using cash, and that other businesses be such that DCF+R is optimized by harvesting market share and generating cash.

Finally, Apollo has identified its greatest corporate strengths to be its marketing and R&D capabilities. Consequently, it prefers to pursue investment opportunities, internal or external, which require those strengths to succeed. This case is reprinted from Alan Cleland, *PIMS Planning Guide: Acquisition Analysis* Cambridge, Mass., Strategic Planning Institute, 1979. Reprinted with permission of the publisher.

Portfolio Analysis Results

In Apollo's case, the portfolio analysis revealed a gap to be filled by businesses which could use cash while gaining share. This imbalance is shown graphically in Exhibit 1. Apollo's long-range corporate plans indicated that this gap would widen over time, as shown in Exhibit 2. A final conclusion of the portfolio analysis was that Apollo's top management did not want to sacrifice intermediate-term ROI drastically while growing in share and using cash to maximize DCF+R. This is shown in Exhibit 3. Any tradeoff between long-term and short-term performance in the shaded area can be achieved with Apollo's existing portfolio of businesses. Movement to a point outside the shaded area requires adding businesses to the portfolio. Apollo desires that the movement from plans to goals should be, as nearly as possible, along the vertical, or constant, ROI line.

Using PIMS models, Apollo completed an industry screen and analysis, and a preliminary candidate screen and analysis. One candidate, Orion Corporation, was tentatively selected as promising. Analysis of Orion's competitors, customers,

EXHIBIT 1
APOLLO INDUSTRIES.

Portfolio is cash heavy. Make an acquisition which can gain market share and use cash, start up new SBU's internally, or pay out to stockholders.

Make an acquisition which can gain market share and use cash, start up new SBU's internally, or pay out to stockholders.

EXHIBIT 2
APOLLO INDUSTRIES: Apollo's portfolio with acquisition.

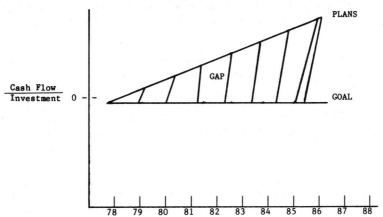

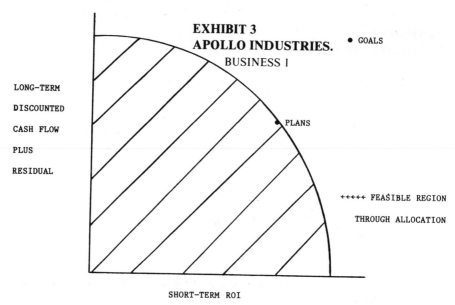

EXHIBIT 3
APOLLO INDUSTRIES.   • GOALS
BUSINESS 1

LONG–TERM
DISCOUNTED
CASH FLOW   • PLANS
PLUS
RESIDUAL

                                     +++++ FEASIBLE REGION
                                     THROUGH ALLOCATION

SHORT–TERM ROI

and suppliers using the LIM (limited information analysis) confirmed this preliminary finding. On this basis, Orion was selected for intensive analysis. Were Orion
to be acquired, it would be with an existing Apollo unit. Consequently, questions
of synergy did not arise.

Orion Corporation: Limited Information (LIM) Analysis

The structure of Orion Corportion, a large, publicly held corporation, is
shown in Exhibit 4. Orion's annual SEC Form 10-K reveals that Orion is comprised

EXHIBIT 4
ORION CORPORATION

BUSINESS 1

BUSINESS 2	BUSINESS 3	BUSINESS 4	BUSINESS 5

Business 1, Orion Corporation, is comprised of businesses 2, 3, 4, and 5.

Businesses 2, 3, 4, 5 are lines of business in the SEC 10-K report sense, and are not
necessarily business units as defined by the Strategic Planning Institute.

EXHIBIT 5
Sequence of analysis ORION CORPORATION.

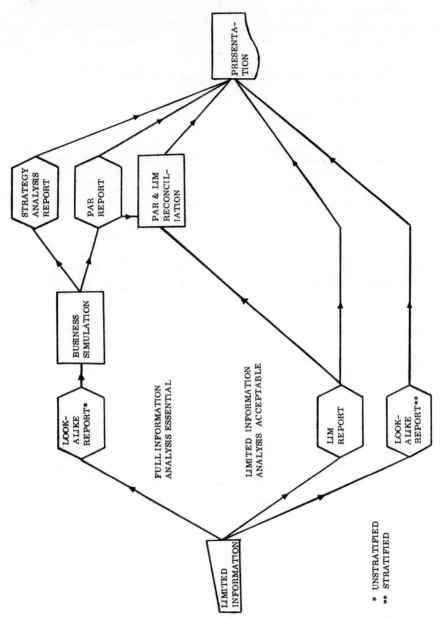

Source: Rochelle O'Connor, Resource Allocation and Strategic Planning, The Conference Board, Information Bulletin No. 99, p. 5.

EXHIBIT 6
ORION CORPORATION
LIM Data

	Factors	PIMS Mean	Business Number				
			1	2	3	4	5
	(COMPETITION POSITION AND ACTIONS FACTORS)						
1.	% Market Share	23.6	25	22	30	28	12
2.	% Relative Market Share	61.7	65	57	60	87	31
3.	Relative Product Quality	25.9	35	40	35	35	30
4.	Relative Price	103.5	101	105	100	100	100
5.	% Employees Unionized	48.3	90	90	90	90	90
6.	% New Products/Sales	11.9	12	20	5	10	30
7.	% R&D Expenses/Sales	2.4	6	8	5	6	7
8.	% Marketing Expenses/Sales	10.8	12	12	12	12	12
	(CAPITAL AND PRODUCTION STRUCTURE FACTORS)						
9.	% Investment/Sales	56.1	72	90	62	73	66
10.	% Investment/Value Added	96.7	121	150	103	121	110
11.	% Fixed-Capital Intensity	52.3	44	44	44	44	44
12.	% Vertical Integration	58.8	60	60	60	60	60
13.	Value/Added/Employees ($1000)	30.0	35	35	35	35	35
14.	% Capacity Utilization	79.6	76	80	80	70	75
	(MARKET ENVIRONMENT FACTORS)						
15.	Real Market Growth Rate	8.2	13	9	20	10	7
16.	% Share of 4 Largest Firms	56.5	65	60	80	60	50
17.	% of Customers = 50% Sales	12.2	9	5	10	10	20
18.	Purchase Amount						
	—Immediate Customers	5.2	6	5	10	10	20
	Sales		100	26	37	28	9
	Actual ROI		18				

of four "lines of business." We stress that these are businesses in the 10-K sense only, and are almost certainly portfolios of business units in the SPI (Strategic Planning Institute) sense. For the balance of this analysis, we will refer to Orion as a whole as business 1, and its four lines of business as businesses 2, 3, 4, and 5, respectively.

The sequence of analysis of the proposed acquisition of Orion is shown schematically in Exhibit 5. The first steps of the analysis are those shown along the bottom branch of the schematic, assuming a limited-information analysis would be acceptable. These involve the LIM report and the use of stratified "look-alikes."

As Exhibit 6 shows, Apollo's management was able to determine directly or to estimate the information about Orion and its four lines of business necessary to run a LIM on each. The bottom of Exhibit 7 indicates that Orion's sales have been disguised to show only the relative magnitude of the lines of business. Business 3 is the largest, with 37 percent of total sales, followed by businesses 4, 2, and 5.

It will be important to remember later in the analysis that Orion's overall pretax, pre-interest ROI is 18 percent. We note that the investment intensity of Orion and each of its lines of business is above the PIMS mean. Real market growth rates are, in general, high, with Business 3 growing at an annual rate of 20 percent.

LIM Analysis

The LIM ROI analysis of Orion and its lines of business is shown in Exhibit 7. The biggest negative impact on ROI is the high investment intensity of Orion. Other negative factors are high R&D and marketing expenses, a high level of unionization, a high purchase amount by immediate customers, and high levels of new products in businesses 2 and 5. These negative factors outweigh the positive factors of reasonably attractive market share and a high level of labor output, as measured by value added per employee. As a result, the estimated ROI for Orion is 11.9 percent, well below both its actual ROI of 18 percent and the PIMS mean ROI of 22.1 percent.

Note that the investment-weighted average LIM ROI of Orion's lines of business is 10.8 percent, quite close to the 11.9 percent figure measured directly. This is the first evidence in the analysis that businesses 2, 3, 4, and 5 may be homogeneous enough with respect to their structural characteristics to be treated as a single unit for purposes of further analysis.

The LIM strategy analysis is shown in Exhibit 8. Remember that Apollo's portfolio need is for a business which can optimize DCF+R by using cash and intermediate-term ROI. Accordingly, a 20 percent share–gain strategy is compared to a continuation of the present strategy under assumptions of a 12 percent real market growth rate and a 3 percent price growth rate.

As shown, in the process of the 20 percent share gain, all businesses use cash without drastically sacrificing ROI in year five. Importantly, however, the LIM strategy analysis has no optimization capability. Thus, we do not know whether share move optimizes DCF+R. This can be determined only with the strategy analysis report (SAR), which requires fuller information to use. We will show how to develop this fuller information shortly, but will first conclude the limited-information analysis using the report on "look-alikes."

Stratified "Look-Alikes" Analysis

The report on "look-alikes" selects a small sample of businesses from the data base with structural characteristics similar to those of Orion Corporation. It shows

EXHIBIT 7 ORION CORPORATION

LIM ROI ANALYSIS

	IMPACT ON BUSINESS NUMBERS				
Factors	*1*	*2*	*3*	*4*	*5*
Competitive Position:					
Market Share }					
Relative Market Share}	1.6	0.7	1.8	2.4	−2.4
Relative Quality	0.7	1.3	0.7	0.8	0.3
Relative Price	−0.1	0.0	−0.1	−0.1	−0.1
% Employees Unionized	−2.6	−2.3	−2.7	−2.9	−1.7
% New Products/Sales	−0.1	−1.1	0.3	0.3	−2.4
R&D Expense/Sales	−2.7	−3.9	−2.6	−2.6	−3.3
Marketing Expense/Sales	−1.0	−1.0	−1.0	−1.0	−1.1
SUBTOTAL	−4.2	−6.3	−3.6	−3.1	−10.7
Capital and Production Structure:					
Investment/Sales }					
Investment/Value Added}	−6.9	−10.4	−4.2	−7.1	−4.8
Fixed Capital Intensity	0.4	0.3	0.3	0.5	0.4
Vertical Integration	0.2	0.2	0.2	0.2	0.2
Value Added/Employee	1.1	1.1	1.1	1.1	1.1
Capacity Utilization	−0.4	0.2	0.2	−1.5	−0.6
SUBTOTAL	−5.6	−8.6	−2.4	−6.8	−3.7

Note: There might be some rounding errors in the process of computations.

LIM MODEL

	IMPACT ON BUSINESS NUMBERS				
Factors	*1*	*2*	*3*	*4*	*5*
Market Environment					
Real Market Growth Rate	0.5	0.3	0.7	0.3	0.1
Share 4 Largest Firms	0.4	0.2	0.9	0.2	−0.2
% Customers = 50% Sales	0.0	0.0	0.0	0.0	0.1
Purchase Amount					
—Immediate Customers	−1.2	−1.2	−1.2	−1.2	−2.8
SUBTOTAL	−0.3	−0.7	0.4	−0.7	−2.8
Total Impact	−10.2	−15.8	−5.7	−10.8	−17.0
Average ROI, All PIMS Business	22.1	22.1	22.1	22.1	22.1
ESTIMATED ROI	11.9	6.3	16.4	11.3	5.1
Weighted Impact* for					
Business 2, 3, 4, and 5	−11.3				
Average ROI, All PIMS Business	22.1				
ESTIMATED ROI	10.8				

*Weighted by Investment

EXHIBIT 8

ORION CORPORATION

LIM MARKET SHARE GAIN STRATEGY IMPLEMENTATION TIME—FIVE YEARS

Assumptions: Real Market Growth: 12%
Selling Price Growth: 3%

Factor:	Business 1		Business 2		Business 3		Business 4		Business 5	
	Present	Build 20%	Present	Build 20%	Present	Build 20%	Present	Build 20%	Present	Build 20%
Market Share (%)	25.7	30.8	22.0	26.4	30.0	36.0	28.0	33.6	12.0	14.4
Relative Market Share (%)	65.0	86.0	52.8	73.5	60.0	78.7	87.5	113.9	31.5	38.9
Relative Product Quality (%)	35.0	38.7	40.0	42.7	35.0	38.7	35.0	38.5	30.0	31.5
Capacity Utilization (%)	76.7	76.7	80.0	80.0	80.0	80.0	70.0	70.0	75.0	75.0
Investment/Value Added (%)	121.0	121.0	150.0	150.0	103.0	103.0	121.0	121.0	110.0	110.0
Investment/Sales (%)	72.7	72.7	90.0	90.0	62.0	62.0	73.0	73.0	66.0	66.0
Fixed-Capital Intensity (%)	44.0	44.0	44.0	44.0	44.0	44.0	44.0	44.0	44.0	44.0
Value Added/Employee ($000)	35.0	35.0	35.0	35.0	35.0	35.0	35.0	35.0	35.0	35.0
Performance Criteria (Year Five)										
Sales	100.0	241.0	26.0	62.8	37.0	89.3	28.0	67.6	9.0	21.7
Net Income	13.1	27.4	4.2	7.0	4.0	10.0	3.7	7.5	1.1	1.8
Investment	72.7	175.5	23.4	56.5	22.9	55.4	20.4	49.3	5.9	14.3
ROI	18.0	15.6	18.0	12.4	18.0	18.1	18.0	15.2	18.0	12.5
Cash Flow		−6.9		−3.1		−1.5		−2.0		−0.8

EXHIBIT 9
ORION CORPORATION
REPORT ON "LOOK-ALIKES"

	Stratification Criterion	Orion
	Return on Investment (Pretax)	18
Weight	Matching Criteria	
6.	Market Share	25.7
6.	Relative Market Share	65.0
4.	Real Product Quality	35.0
1.	Relative Price	101.3
1.	% of Employees Unionized	90.0
2.	% Sales New Products	12.5
2.	Total R&D/Total Revenue	6.2
5.	Marketing Expense/Revenue	12.0
6.	Investment Intensity (I/REV)	72.7
6.	Investment Intensity (I/AVA)	121.0
3.	Fixed-Capital Intensity (GBV/REV)	44.0
2.	Vertical Integration	60.0
4.	Employee Productivity (VA/EMP)	35.0
1.	Capacity Utilization	76.7
1.	Real Market Growth	13.1
1.	Big-4 Market Share	65.0
1.	% Concentration Purchase Immediate Customer	9.6
2.	Purchase Amount Immediate Customer	6.0

how successful businesses within that sample differ from unsuccesful ones. Finally, it raises the question of whether Orion, if acquired, could be made to look more like the successful businesses.

The structural characteristics of Orion used as matching criteria in the search of the data base for similar businesses are shown in Exhibit 9. These are the 18 LIM factors, the totality of the information PIMS Associates was given in making the Orion analysis. They are weighted by their relative importance as profit determinants. The definition of success used as the stratification criterion was ROI, since Apollo wanted to maintain ROI during the share-gain process.

The results of the stratified "look-alikes" analysis are shown in Exhibit 10. At a significance level of 90 percent or higher, the successful businesses had lower R&D expenses and fixed-capital intensity than did either the unsuccessful businesses or Orion. The successful businesses introduced fewer new products relative to competitors than did the unsuccessful businesses, and enjoyed a better ratio of cash flow to investment.

In summary, the questions to be asked are whether to decrease R&D expenses, new product introductions relative to competitors, and fixed-capital

EXHIBIT 10
ORION CORPORATION
REPORT ON "LOOK-ALIKES"

Factor	Orion	12 Closest "Look-Alikes" with ROI* Less than 14.7	12 Closest "Look-Alikes" with ROI† Less than 14.7
Selected Factors Significant at the 90% Level or Higher			
ROI	18.0	5.9	26.2
Total R&D/Sales	6.2	4.8	2.8
Total Marketing/Sales	12.0	9.1	11.4
Relative % New Products		3.7	−2.6
Fixed-Capital Intensity	44.0	57.0	33.1
Cash Flow/Investment		−1.3	4.7

* For unsuccessful businesses
† For successful businesses

intensity, if Orion should be acquired. Efforts should also be untertaken to improve the ratio of cash flow to investment. We will see these signals confirmed later by the SAR. Apollo's management concluded that Orion could probably be made to look more like the successful businesses should it be acquired.

Expanding Limited Information

We saw earlier that one characteristic of acquisition analysis is that it usually must be done under conditions of limited information. The question therefore arises of whether this is acceptable, given the size and importance of Orion relative to Apollo. Apollo asked PIMS Associates to explore ways of expanding these limited data into fuller information.

The upper branch of the schematic in Exhibit 5 shows the method PIMS Associates developed in response to Apollo's request to expand limited information, since Apollo's management felt a full-information analysis was essential. This method of expanding limited information involves the use of unstratified "look-alikes" to obtain a fuller picture of Orion, based on the richness of Strategic Planning Institute's data base. This fuller picture becomes a simulated business on which PIMS full-information reports, PAR and SAR,[1] can be run. It is only through the SAR, with its capacity to show the strategy optimizing DCF+R, that the question of whether Orion could fill the gap in Apollo's portfolio can be answered.

The use of unstratified "look-alikes" analysis to expand limited information is shown in Exhibit 11. The factors shown are the structural characteristics of Orion needed to run PIM's full-information models, PAR and SAR. Selected items of

EXHIBIT 11
ORION CORPORATION
LOOK-ALIKE FACTORS USED FOR THE
FULL INFORMATION SIMULATION OF ORION CORPORATION

Factor	Orion	Average Values for 12 Closest "Look-Alikes"
Description of Business (Form 1)		
Standardization?		0.7
% Concentration Purchase Immediate Customer	9.6	13.4
Purchase Amount Immediate Customer	6.0	5.8
Vertical Integration Backward		1.9
Vertical Integration Forward		2.1
% of Employees Unionized	90.0	55.0
Financial Information (Form 2)		
Income Statement		
Purchases/Total Revenue		41.5
Vertical Integration	60.0	58.5
Manufacturing/Total Revenue		27.6
Total R&D/Total Revenue	6.0	3.7
Marketing Expense/Revenue	12.0	10.4
Manufacturing and Depreciation/Revenue		29.8
Net Income/Revenue		10.5
Balance Sheet		
Receivables/Revenue		21.2
Finished Goods Inventory/Revenue		12.3
RM and WIP Inventory/Revenue		17.6
Fixed-Capital Intensity (GBV/REV)	44.0	40.9
Net Book Value/Revenue		21.2
% Change in Net Book Value		13.2
Newness of Plant Equipment		55.6
Other Form Information		
Replacement Cost/Gross Book Value		207.0
Sales per Employee		48.4
Sales per Salesman		1048.0

Market Information (Form 3)

Relative Product Quality	35.0	38.6
Market Share	25.7	25.1
% Change in Market Share		4.5
Market Share Competitor A		24.8
Market Share Competitor B		14.6
Market Share Competitor C		8.9
Material Cost Growth		10.7
Wage Rate Growth		9.0
Selling Price Growth	3.0	9.2
Served Market Growth (Current $)	13.1	8.9
Real Market Growth		0.8
Real Sales Growth		
Relative Price	101.3	102.7

Factor

% Sales New Products	12.5	12.6
Competitor % New Products		14.2
Relative % New Products		−1.3
Relative Sales Force		2.8
Relative Services		3.5

Projections (Form 5)

Forecast % Change Served Market—Short Term	10.6
Forecast % Change Served Market—Long Term	10.0
Forecast % Change Selling Price—Short Term	6.9
Forecast % Change Selling Price—Long Term	6.4
Forecast % Change Material Cost—Short Term	6.9
Forecast % Change Material Cost—Long Term	6.6
Forecast % Change Wage Rates—Short Term	7.6
Forecast % Change Wage Rates—Long Term	7.1
Discount Rate	9.3
Capital Charge Rate	9.9

information known about Orion are shown and compared to the 12 closest, or unstratified, "look-alikes" in the data base, to give some idea of the goodness of fit between Orion and this simulated, composite business that might be used as a proxy for Orion. The fits between Orion and the simulated business for percentage of purchase concentration of immediate customers, typical purchase amount of immediate customers, vertical integration, marketing expenses/revenue, fixed-capital intensity, quality, market share, relative price, and percentage of sales from new products are reasonably good. The fits between Orion and the simulated business for percentage of employees unionized and total R&D/total revenue are less good. Information regarding the true value of the remaining factors is unavailable.

At this point in the analysis, Apollo's management team had to make a judgment. At one extreme, it could disregard the unstratified "look-alikes" simulation of Orion and conclude the analysis on a limited-information basis. Because of the size and importance of the acquisition relative to Apollo, management was reluctant to do this. At the other extreme, management could accept the simulation in its entirety. This alternative was also rejected because it was apparent that the fit of some factors was less good than of others.

Apollo's management chose a middle course. They chose to simulate Orion by using, first, whatever values were known; second, their own guesses about other factors where they had some basis for guessing; and third, the values from the unstratified "look-alikes" for those factors for whose values they had absolutely no feel. They reasoned that, for this last class of factors, the use of values derived from the 12 closest "look-alikes" in the data base was decidedly better than using the PIMS mean value derived from all 1,500 businesses in the data base. PIMS Associates were requested to proceed with a full-information analysis on this basis.

Orion Corporation: Full-Information Analysis

PAR ROI Analysis

The PAR ROI analysis of Orion is shown in Exhibits 12, 13, and 14. Exhibit 12 reveals that the PAR ROI of 10.1 percent is not much different from the LIM ROI of 11.9 percent. The deviation between the actual ROI of 18 percent and the PAR ROI of 10.1 percent will become important when we consider the pricing of Orion.

Exhibit 13 highlights all of the factors whose impact on PAR ROI is greater than one point of ROI. Investment intensity remains the biggest profit drag. Note that the effect of R&D expenses/sales has increased from −2.7 ROI points in LIM to −5.5 ROI points in the PAR ROI Report. This reflects the PIMS finding that R&D is less profitable to do in high-growth markets such as Orion's, where new products and new technologies are not needed to stimulate demand, than it is in low-growth markets, where such stimulation is indeed needed.

EXHIBIT 12
ORION CORPORATION
PAR ROI REPORT SUMMARY

Category	Impact
Attractiveness of Environment	0.6
Competitive Position	−0.4
Differentiation from Competitors	2.4
Effectiveness of Investment Use	−8.0
Discretionary Budget Expenditures	−6.5
Total Impact	−11.9
PIMS Average ROI	22.0
PAR ROI	10.1
Actual ROI	18.0
PAR ROI	10.1
Deviation from PAR	7.9

Exhibit 14 shows the additional information we have gained about Orion by expanding limited information. We have discovered that an additional strength in Orion's current position is the fact that it makes custom products and that it has a strong long-run growth rate of 20 percent.

We have gained knowledge about its weakness in investment intensity, and now know that it extends to inventory, in addition to fixed capital.

Understanding the Difference between PAR and LIM Analysis

All of the factors and interaction terms in the LIM equation appear in the PAR equation. The greater ROI predictions are excluded from LIM ROI. Those factors and interactions having an impact greater than one ROI point are shown individually in Exhibit 15. In this case, the positive and negative impacts nearly net out, and LIM and PAR ROI are close. If all of the factors had been positive in impact, however, a different conclusion might have been reached than the one we will see shortly regarding both accepting the acquisition and the price to be paid for it.

The last few pages of this planning guide are rather quantitative. This quantification was necessary to expand limited information into fuller information. It was also necessary to see how the current strategic position of the business simulated by unstratified "look-alikes," which we are now using as a proxy for Orion, differs from the position of Orion itself, as shown in the LIM report. Now that we have this fuller picture of Orion, what do we do with it? We use it to make the key decisions about whether Orion will fill the gap in Apollo's portfolio, and

EXHIBIT 13
ORION CORPORATION
PAR ROI REPORT

	PIMS Mean	This Business	Impact
Attractiveness of Environment			0.6
Purchase Amount—Immediate Costs	5.2	6.0	−1.3
Real Market Growth, Short Run	8.2	13.1	0.8
Industry (SIC) Growth, Long Run	9.1	20.1	1.1
Selling Price Growth Rate	6.8	6.1	−0.1
Competitive Position			−0.4
Market Position			1.4
Market Share	23.7	25.0	
Relative Market Share	61.7	65.8	
Industry Concentration Ratio	56.5	65.0	0.4
Employees Unionized (%)	48.3	90.0	−1.6
Immediate Customer Fragmentation	12.2	12.0	−0.0
Market Share Growth Rate	3.3	0.0	−0.5
Market Share Instability	4.0	0.0	−0.0
Differentiation from Competitors			2.4
Relative Product Quality	25.9	35.0	0.8
Price Relative to Competition	103.5	101.3	−0.2
Standard Products/Services?		NO	1.6
Relative Compensation	100.9	102.5	0.2
New-Product Sales/Total Sales	11.9	12.5	−0.1
Effectiveness of Investment Use			−8.0
Investment Intensity			−6.9
Investment/Sales	56.1	73.9	
Investment/Value Added	96.7	122.7	
Value Added per Employee ($000)	30.0	35.1	1.0
Vertical Integration	58.8	60.1	0.2
Relative Integration Backward		SAME	0.1
Relative Integration Forward		SAME	−0.3
Fixed-Capital Intensity	52.3	44.0	0.4
Capacity Utilization	79.6	76.7	−0.4
Investment per Employee ($000)	30.4	43.1	0.2
Inventory/Sales	18.8	30.0	−2.4
FIFO Valuation?	55.0	NO	0.0
Newness of P&E (NBV/GBV)		50.3	0.1
Discretionary Budget Expenditures			−6.5
Marketing Expense/Sales	10.8	12.0	−1.0
R&D Expense/Sales	2.4	6.0	−5.5

EXHIBIT 14
ORION PAR REPORT SUMMARY

This business's strengths are:

   1. Strong market position
   2. Productive workforce (Value Added/ Employee)
 *3. Long-run (SIC) growth of 20%
 *4. The fact that it makes custom products

This business's weaknesses are:

   1. High level of unionization
   2. High R&D expense
   3. High marketing expense
   4. High level of investment intensity
   5. Immediate customers purchase in large amounts
 *6. High levels of inventories

  *Additional strengths and weaknesses revealed in full information analysis.

what price should be paid for Orion if it does. These decisions can be made with the SAR. This is why we have gone to great lengths to develop the information required to use it.

Pricing Acquisition Candidates

An increasing number of corporations are using the discounted cash flow approach chosen by Apollo for pricing acquisitions.[2] Under this method, the price

EXHIBIT 15
ORION CORPORATION
PAR AND LIM RECONCILIATION

Factors in PAR, Not in LIM	
Industry (SIC) growth, long run	1.1
Products not standardized	1.6
Inventory/ Sales	−2.4
Interaction in PAR, Not in LIM	
Unionization * Industry growth, LR	−2.5
R&D Sales * Industry Growth, LR	−3.3
Other	3.7
Difference	−1.8
LIM ROI	11.9
PAR ROI	10.1
Difference	−1.8

173

of an acquisition candidate should be the present value of its net cash flow, plus the value of any assets on the balance sheet not required to generate this stream of net cash flow, less debt.

The logic in using this approach is that it puts the analysis of external capital expenditures, which acquisitions represent, on the same basis as the analysis of internal capital expenditures, which have long been analyzed using discounted cash flow techniques. By avoiding an earnings per share approach, it properly separates the investment from the financing decision. This analysis concentrates on the portfolio investment decision, leaving the financing decision to be made separately as part of capital structure analysis. PIMS Associates can also price acquisitions on the basis of discounted net income or ROI for member companies which prefer to use these criteria.

Apollo's management recognized that there were three benefits in using PIMS and SAR to arrive at a price to be paid for Orion using the discounted cash flow criterion:

1. PIMS net cash flow projections are based on structural characteristics of the company acquired, not a straight-line extrapolation or "hockey-stick" projection of past results.
2. The net cash flow benefit of moving from Orion's current trajectory to an optimum strategy (in this case, DCF+R) can be quantified.
3. The net cash flow benefit or penalty of assuming that Orion moves from its actual to its PAR ROI can be quantified.

Orion Corporation: Pricing

Strategy Reports

Pricing considerations for Orion Corporation are shown in Exhibit 16. Numbers in the table are the values of DCF+R taken from the SAR. Four alternative scenarios are shown in the rows. The first two rows show values for a "no planned change" strategy under the assumptions that deviation from PAR ROI diminishes and that deviation from PAR ROI remains constant, respectively. The last two rows show the same assumptions for the strategy to optimize DCF+R. The columns show values of DCF+R for each of the businesses.

The column headed Σ 2...5 is the sum of DCF+R for businesses 2, 3, 4, and 5, Orion's four lines of business. In computing DCF+R values for these businesses, the same technique of using unstratified "look-alikes" to expand limited information was used as shown earlier for Orion Corporation (business 1). If this technique of expanding limited information were perfect, column 1 would equal Σ 2...5 in each row. Given the fact that each limited information expansion was done independently, the values in the two columns are quite close. This gives us confidence, once again, that this experimental technique of expanding limited information holds promise, and that PIMS models can be applied to the analysis of portfolios of reasonably homogeneous businesses, as well as to individual business units.

EXHIBIT 16
ORION CORPORATION
LIM Data

	Business Number					
	1	*Σ2...5*	*2*	*3*	*4*	*5*
No Planned Change						
Deviation from PAR ROI diminishes	738	658	138	259	226	35
Deviation from PAR ROI remains constant	1139	1041	333	277	320	111
Optimize DCF + Residual Value						
Deviation from PAR ROI diminishes	1393	1743	449	521	399	104
Deviation from PAR ROI remains constant	1831	1807	564	531	497	215

1) The sum of the parts is surprisingly close to the whole, given the experimental information "Look-Alike" transformation from limited to full information.

2) The price to be paid for the acquisition would be between 1393 and 1831, assuming the absence of severable assets or debt.

3) Benefit of moving from a No Planned Change strategy to an optimum strategy is quantified:

    A. $1393 - 738 = 655$ Assuming deviation decay
    B. $1831 - 1139 = 692$ Assuming no decay

4) Value penalty of moving toward PAR is quantified:

    A. $1139 - 738 = 401$ Assuming a No Planned Change Strategy
    B. $1831 - 1393 = 438$ Assuming a DCF + R Optimization Strategy

5) The net impact of both optimization and decay is quantified:

$$1393 - 1139 = \underline{\underline{254}}$$

Each of the three advantages of using PIMS in pricing acquisitions is shown. First, the present values of DCF+R are all based on the structural characteristics of the respective businesses, not extrapolations of past results. The suggested maximum price to be paid for Orion is between $1.393 billion and $1.831 billion, using a 10 percent discount rate and assuming no severable assets or debt on Orion's balance sheet. This price range would indicate an earnings multiple of between 9.0 times and 11.8 times Orion's estimated $155 million earnings for the current year. If these figures seem high, remember that a corporation of Orion's size could easily have $1 billion of debt on the balance sheet. Second, the benefit of moving from a no planned change strategy to an optimization strategy is quantified. Third, the penalty of assuming that Orion moves from its 18 percent actual ROI to its 10.1 percent PAR ROI is quantified.

EXHIBIT 17
ORION CORPORATION
TEN-YEAR DISCOUNTED CASH FLOWS
UNDER ALTERNATIVE SCENARIOS

No Planned Change

Full Decay	−2992
No Decay	−2591

Optimize DCF + Residual Value

Full Decay	−748
No Decay	−1439

1) The negative cash flows here show that all of the value we saw in Exhibit 17 is in the residual. This confirms our earlier LIM analysis, where all of the cash flows in Year 5 were negative.

2) Remember, in the "Look-Alike" analysis, cash flow was significant at the 90% level.

The net impact of the second and third factors is $1.393 billion minus $1.139 billion, or $254 million. This means that should a bidding war for Orion develop, Apollo Industries could justify paying $254 million more for Orion than a non-member could, by reason of the knowledge gained through Apollo's PIMS membership.

Clearly, all the figures above should be understood as approximations. They were simply read from the SAR, and should not be interpreted as implying greater exactitude than the broad directional signals which the model builders intended the SAR to convey.

Components of Orion's Value

An interesting insight into the components of Orion's value is shown in Exhibit 17. The negative present values of ten-year cash flows show that all of the value in the DCF+R figures in Exhibit 16 comes from an extremely high residual value. For example, the residual in the DCF+R-optimizing strategy, assuming the deviation from PAR ROI disappears, would be $1.439 billion + $0.748 billion, or $2.187 billion. Some might interpret the fact that all of Orion's value arises from its year-ten residual value as signifying a risky investment. Remember, however, that Apollo wanted a vehicle that used cash. The SAR confirms the LIM conclusion that Orion certainly would accomplish this.

It is also worth remembering that the stratified "look-alikes" analysis showed that successful "look-alikes" used less cash than the unsuccessful ones. This is also confirmed in Exhibit 17, where the optimum strategy uses less cash than the no planned change strategy.

EXHIBIT 18
ORION CORPORATION
DETAIL OF STRATEGY MOVE:
OPTIMIZE 10-YEAR DISCOUNTED CASH FLOW + RESIDUAL VALUE

	Starting Position 1977	Implementation of Strategy 1979	New Steady State Position 1982	New Long Term Position 1987
Strategic Position				
Market Share	25%	22%	15%	15%
Vertical Integration	60%	64%	72%	72%
Mechanization	56%	52%	44%	44%
Financial Results:				
Return on Investment	18%	21%	13%	12%
Return on Sales	13%	15%	10%	13%
Typical Support Tactics:				
Relative Quality of Service	3.0	2.9	2.8	2.8
Relative Product Quality	35%	25%	−3%	15%
% New Products	13%	7%	1%	6%
Marketing/Sales	12%	9.6%	7.3%	6.6%
R&D/Sales	6%	5.2%	5.3%	3.0%
Finished Goods Inventory/Sales	13.5%	11.9%	7.7%	14.1%
Backlog/Sales	0%	0%	0%	0%

Details of the strategy move to optimize DCF+R for Orion Corporation, assuming that actual ROI approaches PAR ROI, as shown in Exhibit 18, follow. We see that the supporting tactics confirm the signals which appeared earlier in the stratified "look-alikes" analysis. These signals were to decrease new products and the ratio of R&D to sales. The financial results show that ROI is not drastically reduced, but does decline from 18 percent to 12 percent with time as actual ROI approaches PAR ROI.

Regarding strategic position, we see that mechanization declines from 56 percent to 44 percent, confirming the stratified "look-alikes" suggestion to decrease fixed-capital intensity. Most importantly, the optimization strategy calls for a harvest of market share decrease from 25 percent to 15 percent, rather than a growth of market share. Among the factors eliciting the harvest signal are the served market is growing rapidly, capacity must be added quickly and in large increments, and PAR ROI is relatively low. These factors require large amounts of

EXHIBIT 19
ORION CORPORATION
DCF + R OPTIMIZATION STRATEGIES: INDICATED SHARE MOVES

	Business Number				
	1	*2*	*3*	*4*	*5*
Actual ROI approaches PAR ROI	H	H	H	H	G

H = Harvest   G = Grow

1) Remember, the portfolio gap called for a vehicle which could gain market share and use cash.

2) PIMS research shows a tendency for a business's actual ROI to move toward its PAR ROI over time.

3) Assuming actual ROI of Orion Corporation moves toward its PAR ROI, the strategy to optimize Discounted Net Income plus residual calls for harvesting, rather than growing, market share.

fixed and working capital to maintain, let alone grow, market position. We just saw that large amounts of cash were required even though the position was being harvested. The analysis in Exhibit 19 of the SAR for each of Orion's lines of business shows that harvesting is indicated for all except the smallest.

A final line of inquiry would be to determine under what circumstances the SAR might give a signal to gain share under a DCF+R optimization. Without quantifying this example, we note that the present value of the residual would have to increase by more than the present value of the greatly increased ten-year cash outflows that such a strategy would entail. Otherwise, there would be no justification for investing this substantial additional cash. The SAR shows that, under an aggressive share strategy, the increase in terminal value falls far short of the increase in cash outflows.

Conclusion and Summary

It appears that Orion will not fill the gap in Apollo's portfolio. Apollo's goal is to maximize shareholder wealth, and it believes this can be done by optimizing the present value of cash flow for each business in its portfolio. Apollo also wants to maintain a portfolio balance between business units which generate cash while harvesting share. The gap in Apollo's portfolio called for a business which could use cash while gaining share. Orion Corporation uses cash while harvesting share. Since Orion does not fill the portfolio gap, the acquisition should be rejected despite its relatedness in marketing and R&D intensity, and its capacity to use cash. The indicated harvest of market share would leave it in a weak strategic position in comparison with its competitors in this rapidly growing market.

The acquisition decision is a portfolio decision. It can be made on a sound basis only at the conclusion of a portfolio study identifying the gap between corporate goals and the contribution the business units currently comprising the portfolio can make toward attaining these goals. The contribution required to fill this gap from business units not yet a part of the portfolio becomes apparent. The search can now begin for an acquisition candidate with the potential to make this contribution. PIMS can help at each step of the process.

NOTES

1. While the PAR report focuses on what profit rate, cash flow and other items are "normal" for the combination of normal circumstances, SAR deals with what would happen (short-term and long-term) if certain strategic changes are made.

2. "The Cash-Flow Takeover Formula," *Business Week*, December 18, 1978, pp. 86–87.

Strategic Budgeting for Small
and Medium-Size Firms
——8——

Poor or inadequate financial planning and management, plus a lack of resources, are the chief causes of small business failures. In fact, many of the more significant reasons, which include deficient planning, over-investment, unrealistic pricing, low sales, and inadequate cost control can be attributed to the small business manager's ignorance of events inside and outside his door.[1] All too often, the daily routine consumes the lion's share of the owner/manager's time and energy, leaving no time for "stargazing." However, these threats to success are all too real to ignore, and a strategic orientation is thus critical.

Strategy is defined as managerial planning designed to adapt a small firm to its external environment in a manner perceived to achieve sales and profit goals.[2] Yet the techniques most frequently found involve procedures for such planning that, because of their complexity, might discourage the manager contemplating their use in a small organization. As a result, many small firms in genuine need of strategic planning do not use this management aid.[3] The consequence of this fact is that most companies and people do not realize their full potential because all their time is taken up with the urgent tasks at hand. Attending to the "merely urgent"—today's crisis—will seldom yield the right results because it imposes a priority on activities that is not optimal.[4] Planning develops a sense of the truly important and builds upon direction and scope. Tactical planning is first-order change within a functioning system; it helps a company do what it already does, only better. Strategic planning, however, implies second-order change—to the system itself.[5]

For the most part, current literature directed to small businesses falls mainly into two classes: extremely theoretical or extremely basic.[6] Should small business managers be tempted to copy corporate planning techniques? No, since copying the strict form of a technique—instead of its function—is usually inefficient, often ineffective, and has the potential for disaster.[7]

There are three reasons why planning techniques must be uniquely adapted to small firms. First, small businesses lack the financial and human resources that are often required by conventional techniques. Second, small firms usually possess a "personality" orientation rather than the systems approach of the large firm. Finally, the greatest asset of the small business lies in its flexibility and maneuverability.[8]

These factors combine in such a way as to demand practical methods that are nontrivial, yet take advantage of the responsiveness and people orientation of the small firm. This chapter will attempt to describe the environmental issues of small business planning as well as its essential elements and processes. Next there is a brief survey of some planning techniques, and finally an assessment of small firms' options in this area.

ENVIRONMENTAL ISSUES

A Small Business Is Not a Little Big Business

Among many managers, a traditional assumption has been that small businesses should be guided by the same principles of management as the large firm, but on a smaller scale. However, the very size of small businesses leads to a special condition—referred to as resource poverty—that distinguishes them from their bigger counterparts, and necessitates quite different management approaches.[9] Studies have shown that successful planning in small firms is quite different from that of large firms in three important ways.[10]

First, successful small-firm planning is relatively informal, and has a short time horizon. It apparently is better to plan more often for briefer duration than the opposite, and such an approach must be spare on paperwork and procedure. This is not to say that it need not be methodical, however. Second, the focus of the planning is more basic, though not trivial. Functional areas such as finance, promotion, production, and inventory should receive attention as realistic opportunities are pursued and pressing problems are alleviated. All actions must be mutually supportive. Third, as resources within the firm are constrained, the use of outside assistance can make the difference. Such outsiders can be bankers, lawyers, accountants, or consultants.

These elements will all minimize the effect of resource poverty, which results from various conditions found in the smaller company.[11] One factor is the clustering of small businesses in highly fragmented industries, such as wholesaling, retailing, services, and job shops. Competition here focuses on price, and profits are quickly eroded. Another factor is the proportion of revenues represented by the owner's salary. This means that little is left to pay other managers or employees with special skills. Thus, small firms lack some managerial and operational functions. Finally, external forces tend to have greater impact on small businesses than on large ones. Changes wrought by the government or competition have an exaggerated effect on the small, undiversified firm. such limitations mean that small businesses can seldom survive mistakes or bad judgment in all but the insignificant case.

Owner-management of a small business is a special discipline characterized by severe constraints. For the small firm, liquidity must be a prime objective and is at the heart of strategic planning and budgeting. Most small companies do best with conservative growth rates supported by an owner-manager who possesses a generalist's broad thinking. In contrast with the large firm, the direction of planning must be away from needless sophistication and back to basics.[12]

Planners and Nonplanners

Two essential preconditions are necessary for successful planning: a basic desire to improve upon your current state, and an ability and willingness to change.[13] The owner-manager must desire improvements and be willing to accept change as a way of accomplishing those improvements.

In a study by David Jones,[14] planners and nonplanners were differentiated along several dimensions, including use of market research, long-term forecasting, restrictiveness and predictability of environment, use of short-term plans, search for investment opportunities, and participation in growth strategy.

The planners viewed the environment as being more restrictive, yet felt it was more predictable, than did nonplanners. Planners also made much more use of all the planning activities contained in the Jones study. It seems that planners are also more likely to engage in group consultation rather than make decisions alone. Measured by return on assets, planners were more successful than nonplanners.

Planning firms are likely to take advantage of the desirable aspects of group decision making. These include greater knowledge of the issues, better comprehension, and a better chance of acceptance of the resulting plan. Overall, the planning firm is dynamic, engaged in scanning the environment for opportunities, identifying future trends through research, and involving many members of the organization in the process.

The Importance of Control

Before there can be planning, there must be a structure through which to plan. Some basis in finance and accounting will always be found within that structure, and frequently the act of planning assures the soundness of the basic structures by making active use of them, focusing upon their behavior, and otherwise placing substantial reliance upon them. The nonplanning firm will frequently find trouble when critical parts of this interlocking structure are ignored or abused.[15]

Common financial pitfalls for the small business may be categorized as related to capital sufficiency, debt management, cash-flow management, growth management, credit management, and accounting.[16] While some of these traps will spring even on the conscientious planner, the forward thinking and budget preparation that go into creation of a strategic plan will force the owner-manager to consider them.

When forecasting is in a very early stage, at the start of a business, sufficient capital to cover the period between the beginning of investment/expense flows and generation of a profit is essential. Frequently this is overlooked if there is not some kind of written plan. So, too, is the requirement for working capital—which is needed to support sales growth and too often is found through acquiring debt.

In the drive to increase sales, the risk-return tradeoff may not be seen, for a nonplanner drives up volume at the expense of some measure of profitability, such as ROI. It should be recalled that activity and profitability are not always the same thing; a frequent fault of small companies is underestimating costs that change in unexpected ways as volumes increase.[17]

Having a sound financial plan is of critical importance and is reemphasized in such areas as cash budgeting, inventory control, and working-capital analysis. In a study of 143 firms that failed in the Chicago area, 77 percent ceased operating for planning-related shortcomings.[18] A naive owner-manager will frequently confound cash with net income and proceed to remove it from the business. Because of their size, small firms depend upon reinvestment earnings for growth, and frequently fail to build an adequate capital cushion out of retained profits.

When dealing with credit issues, the small business owner-manager will often lose in two ways.[19] First, he/she will fail to cultivate the needed working relationship with a bank officer. It pays to keep your contact primed with the latest performance data on your business, since banks dislike surprises. Second, the customers of a new business often receive credit too easily as that business tries to build sales.

Of course, many problems that beset small businesses have to do with basic accounting. The study by Clute identified 85 percent of the failures studied as having one or more types of accounting difficulties.[20] These range from no (or an incompetent) accountant to inadequate billing and accounts payable systems. Many businesses in trouble had grossly inadequate accounting systems.

To summarize, control is a central issue to the health and survival of a business. Appropriate accounting methods and systems will assure that the information needed for control is present and sets the stage for successful planning. It is to this topic that the discussion now turns.

STRATEGIC PLANNING CHARACTERISTICS

Stages of Business Decision Making

Regardless of firm size, the process of strategic planning has evolved over time. Developing from intuition and crisis management to specialized analysis and computer-based support systems, stages of decision making can be delineated.[21] While the stage of highest development and sophistication defines the forefront of strategic planning, examining a cross-section of businesses will show a correlation between size and decision-making stage. Small firms tend to be in the earlier stages, while larger firms are likely to be at the higher end of the scale.

A definition is now in order for the term "small firm.' The trillion-dollar-plus per year American economy consists of approximately 10 million firms. About 98 percent of these concerns employ fewer than 50 people.[22] It is more to this segment of the economy that this discussion is addressed, although other definitions of "small firms" are used in the literature.[23] Such alternative definitions tend to identify "larger" small firms with a coincidence of greater sophistication.[24] However, the idea presented is that as firms grow, their planning must become more sophisticated. Another point is that as decision-support technology becomes less expensive and more accessible, it tends to infiltrate ever-smaller firms. This allows them to shift their level of sophistication upward without the concurrent growth in employees and sales one might otherwise expect. An interesting study would be the exploration of the effects that this infusion of technology has on the growth of small firms. The earliest stage of business decision making is, as mentioned, intuitive. Such planning places minimal demands on company resources and has a very short time horizon. Little time is required to formulate such plans, and only the business experience of the owner-manager is brought to bear on the day-to-day issues being considered. Its appear to the smallest of businesses can be appreciated—however, as the reader may now appreciate, more is needed.

The owner-manager needs to be directed toward a more rational and systematic process that involves a general analysis and forecast of the situation. He/she must then develop alternatives, make choices, and design implementations.[25] Such is the description of "stage II" decision making. It is a more moderate user of business resources than more advanced planning systems, yet achieves a longer (one- to three-year) time horizon than its predecessor stage. More time is required than stage I, yet it does not need the specialized skills found in stage III strategic planning. Mostly what is required of the planner/decision maker is self-discipline. The issues addressed relate to markets, products, services, and finance. The analysis and forecasting involved present the entrepreneur with identifying and evaluating circumstances that influence a decision or situation in a way compatible with his/her skills. It must emphasize logical, realistic analysis, not "sophisticated" data manipulation.[26]

Key Elements in the Strategic Planning Process

Although a logical and structured analysis is a precondition to systematic decision making, there are many problems awaiting the would-be planner.[27] The rational model may be too ambitious an effort for the owner-manager, since he/she will often possess an incomplete understanding of the state of the environment that affects the firm. Second, goals are often poorly defined, are inexact, and deal only with first-order change within a very short time horizon. Finally, the owner-manager may be unable to determine the full range of alternatives open to choice.

All this would seem to beg the question, however, for these are good reasons to plan. To the extent to which these problems can be reduced, the planning activity will have been successful. As a measurement of success, there are certain questions whose answers can be examined to evaluate a firm's planning effort.[28] They determine a firm's ability to anticipate absolute changes in the firm's own gross sales, relative changes of gross sales compared with those of competitors in the local industry, absolute changes in the firm's own profit, and specific adjustments in the firm's operation to accommodate (or offset) anticipated changes in sales and profit. Only when a firm can respond to all four is it said to be performing strategic planning.

So what does planning do? It seeks to establish objectives, set priorities, validate objectives, and convert activity into results.[29] These are certainly ambitious goals, and they cannot be achieved without the presence of key elements in the planning process.

The first of these elements is a definition of the business. Three questions should be asked by the planner: What is our business now? What will it be in the future? What should it be?[30] Such questions set the boundaries of the firm's operations and set the stage for strategic planning.

A second element is the determination of a sensible planning horizon. The chances are that planning is centered on the annual budget. However, long-range strategic planning is more concerned about the future state of present events or activities. Thus, the small-firm planner needs to focus on a distinct horizon that synchronizes with the operating cycles of the firm and industry.

Another element in the planning process is the establishment of goals and objectives. "Objective" designates a broad strategic aim for the enterprise that expresses management's fundamental intentions and provides guidelines for the future development of the firm.[32] "Goal" identifies a milestone on the path toward the objective. The owner-manager should use quantitative and qualitative statements to direct the efforts of the company. When resources are compared with objectives, it will quickly become apparent if there are any gaps between required and on-hand resources. In this way, the objectives can be modified, resources can be acquired, or both. Systematic long-range planning can minimize these gaps over time with the use of the smallest possible amount of resources. While dissenters to small-firm goal setting say it is meaningless without an understanding of underlying conditions, at some point it makes sense to establish financial and functional goals that are firmly grounded in reality.

A fourth element is the evaluation of distinctive competence. This self-evaluation asks, "What does the firm do well?" A realistic appraisal of present and future strengths and weaknesses is essential in obtaining the proper match between a company's capabilities and its goals and objectives. In general, such things as human and financial resources, plant and equipment, product lines, materials, and patent/trademark positions and capabilities are assessed.[33]

A very critical element in the planning process is environmental analysis. Also called "environmental scanning," this function usually receives a great deal of attention in the large firm, and its treatment by the small firm is a source of concern if strategic planning is to be successful.[34] Choosing a cost-effective technique is by no means impossible, however. Using structured analysis, the small firm can consider the quality and precision of data provided, the firm's need for this type of data, the cost/benefit ratio for this data, and the risk/return trade-off represented by the scanning data.[35]

The environment provides the framework within which the firm operates, and may create opportunities or pose threats. Special attention must be paid to environmental developments with the greatest potential for effecting change. Tracking changes that might pose threats is relatively simple. Perceiving a latent opportunity created by an environmental change is quite a different matter. Moyer suggests the following approach for the small firm on a restricted budget:[36] assign appropriate functional management (perhaps an assistant to the owner-manager) to tracking the two or three developments judged to have the greatest potential impact on the firm, trace the effect on the firm of recurrent environmental developments (business cycles), conduct in-house research (at minimum cost) on environmental forces judged likely to affect the firm's welfare, use outside tracking services, keep top management informed on current business events, and feed back to functional management information on recent developments in their specialties of which they may not be aware.

A sixth element in the strategic plan is a competitive analysis, which asks the traditional questions of comparisons from the perspective of the customers, relative strengths and weaknesses, and so forth. Of importance to the small firm, however, is the fact that the availability of data and the resources with which to analyze it are limited. Dun & Bradstreet and Moody's reports may shed light on the state of incorporated competitors. Other data may be gathered from the planner's own staff. Credit and finance personnel may have useful information, and the value of the sales force should not be overlooked in this regard.[37]

The final element in small-firm strategic planning is a customer analysis. Often, the data for customer analysis are available within the firm, from sales, or externally obtained as part of environmental scanning (demography, economic trends). Questions to answer include the following:[38] Where do customers buy the product? What about the product appeals to the customer? What sales changes are expected? What unique opportunities exist in market segments that can be identified? It is essential to translate changes in the customers' set environment into the small firm's strategic plan.

Steps to Small-Firm Strategic Budgeting

Rather than employing the dynamic planning process described by House,[39] with its large-firm, top-down flow, a "phasing" approach to strategic plan implementation such as that of Robinson may be more appropriate (see Table 8.1). This approach breaks the implementation down into more manageable and logical segments of activity that should appear to the resource-constrained owner-manager. In phasing there are three distinct logical segments: analysis, alternatives/choice, implement/monitor. This is not dissimilar to the decision-making model described by Nagel,[40] in which "signals" are used to feed forward to both data-ordering and current forecast functions. After the output of the ordering is subjected to comparison (with competition), it feeds a selection function (based on distinctive analysis). Both the selection function and current forecast are used to design alternatives for action. Choices are then made and, in effect, the process is repeated.

Phase I activities comprise some of the elements discussed earlier. Analysis is first performed with an internal focus. Analysis of distinctive strengths and weaknesses, resources and capabilities should occur first. Next is external analysis, which explores the areas referred to as the environment. The third step is a competitor analysis, which compares the firm's strengths and weaknesses with those of its direct competitors.

"Alternatives/choice" is the name given to phase II. It seeks first to prioritize internal weaknesses and external threats for which there must be some response before other action can take place. Next is the evaluation of internal strengths and external opportunities. Following these assessments, the owner-manager and other planners will be in a position to brainstorm on how to maximize internal strengths in order to seize external opportunities and minimize the downside risk of internal weaknesses and external threats. This is akin to designing alternatives, which must be made specific for this process to function. The final element of this phase is the act of choosing actions from among simple alternatives.

Prioritizing the chosen actions is the first step in the final phase. The planner should record such decisions in a timetable for later reference and follow-up. Of course, the most critical actions should take place first. Now that the small firm has progressed into the implementation phase, monitoring must commence. Brainstorming should continue with key sources of information, such as partners/functional managers, bankers, accountants, and consultants. Effectiveness measures (hopefully chosen during phase II) should now be evaluated to act as a feedback for control.

Often (if not always) fairly detailed budgets will be prepared, even at a very summarized level for the smallest of firms.[41] For the more sophisticated

TABLE 8.1. Phase approach to strategic planning.

Phase I Analysis	Phase II Alternatives/Choice	Phase III Implement/Monitor
1. Internal focus—evaluation of firm's strengths and weakness in finance, marketing, facilities, location, management, services or product, pricing, cost, customer relations, image, etc.	1. Identification of critical internal weaknesses or external threats that must be met before other action can be taken	1. Commit actions to priority and time table
2. External focus—evaluation of opportunities and threats in particular industry, regional market, sources of capital, economy, technology, and regulation	2. Identification of unusual strengths or external opportunities that must quickly be exploited	2. Begin efforts toward most critical first
3. Competition focus—evaluation of firm's comparative standing with direct competitors: comparison of strengths and weaknesses from above relative to specific competitors within identified external situation	3. Brainstorming generation of ideas/actions that maximize internal strengths to meet external opportunities and minimize impact of internal weaknesses or external threats	3. Continue brainstorming discussion with key information sources: partner, banker, accountant, competitors, supplies, SBDC
	4. Move from general to specific very early in process	4. Identify effectiveness measures of individual actions, such as occupancy rate
	5. Identify simple alternatives	5. Systematically monitor measures
	6. Choose actions	

Source: Reprinted from Richard Robinson, "Forecasting and Small Business," *Journal of Small Business Management,* July 1979, p. 22. Reprinted with permission from *Journal of Small Business Management.*

small firm, these budgets may be associated with projects within programs designed to accomplish certain goals and objectives. The budget schedules will likely include a sales forecast, pro-forma income statement and balance sheet, an estimated sources and uses of funds statement, a cash budget, a capital expenditures budget, and manpower/materials forecasts. By completing these documents, the company will be able to lay out its plans, monitor accomplishments (and failures), trace any critical measures of vitality (liquidity?), and modify plans, programs, and projects through the feedforward/feedback loop.[42]

The Growing Importance of Computers

In the 1980s technology has made quantum leaps forward, especially in terms of the greater power and lower cost of computing. Such change has not been lost on the public, as manufacturers saturate the media with their advertising. Apple, Atari, IBM, and many others push for expanded use of small computers for business and in the home.

For many small companies, this has led to the emergence of computer-based planning models.[43] Originally they may have been used for simple examinations of manufacturing costs or cash flow. Ultimately the models have became the cornerstone of planning for the efficient producer. Frequently referred to as decision support systems (DSS), these computer-based tools add a new dimension to analyzing all sorts of projections prior to making business decisions.[44] Previously beyond the capability of small business owner-managers, management information can now be readily generated to aid in assessing the effects of various outcomes.

Although it is not mandatory for models of certain types, such as a DSS, to be computerized, this approach is essential to processing data on alternative possible outcomes in an efficient and effective way. Without a computer to do the number crunching, small businessmen may abandon their analysis soon after the development of their base case. A small business may not have a computer of its own, yet it can gain access to one and experienced help, in several ways.[45] Its accounting firm, a consultant, a timesharing network or a government or quasi-government agency can help in the task of implementation.

Early in the 1970s it became apparent that to survive tough times, many small firms would have to stop ignoring the capabilities of the computer.[46] As late as 1976, independent businessmen were still ignoring the computer as a way to develop the information necessary for planning and control.[47] Even a casual look through recently published literature will reveal that such a reluctance to embrace technology persists. As firms move toward the later stages of decision making, the computer will play a larger role, yet many businesses today do not have the internal resources to do this level of planning. But this is not to say that there are not more general techniques that can help. Quite the contrary is true.

Basic Tools for Planning

The small enterprise must master venturing to survive and grow, and perceive early indications of success or failure. Benchmark planning data are required but not readily available in a usable form. One technique that is potentially valuable to the small firm focuses on three critical success measures: profitability, cash flow, and capital productivity.[48] Together, these elements can comprise a method of evaluation and a building block in the planning process.

Profitability can be measured by the amount of net earnings per dollar of business assets. These data are available from a special government tabulation made in the mid-1970s.[49] Unfortunately, this measure is not stable over time, as the economy moves through the business cycle. Nevertheless, as a rough estimate, it may provide insight into profitability planning by marking a minimum profit goal for the small-business owner-manager. Such data are available for many asset sizes and industry types. If the enterprise cannot match the average earnings per dollar of assets for others in its industry class and size, then the funds might be better invested elsewhere.

For cash-flow planning, a rough estimate of cash flow by industry group and size is also possible. By adding data on depreciation allowances from the Federal Trade Commission to the earnings data mentioned above, a measure of average cash flow is obtained. The advantage of cash-flow planning is that it imposes the discipline of a cash budget and forces the firm to deal with adequate record keeping. It forces the owner-manager to combine the net effect of operations on the balance sheet and income statement. Since a recurrent weakness of small business is undue attention to accrual-basis profit on the income statement, such a combined emphasis prevents unwise expansion of a business beyond its capital sufficiency.[50]

Enterprises grow over time, and as they do, capital is required. When the timing is correct for such a move, the entrepreneur should have some historical standards by which to compare the firm's capital performance against the norm. Such data are available for small, proprietary, and larger corporate businesses.[51] By combining these measures, the firm can gauge its own performance in a comparative framework.

These measures can be combined with a simple, bottom-up approach to profit planning, called the executive's operational guide.[52] This tool shows the owner-manager what his/her sales and profit should be in the coming year in order to provide an adequate measure of profitability. Further, it overcomes two frequent objections to such planning: the cost to develop and the uncertainty of sales forecasts.

Because the data come from the regular bookkeeping system, cost is nominal. Sales data need only be "reasonable" to provide an operating target.

There are six steps to the program:

1. Analyze costs. Are they variable or fixed? Although many accountants will object to this arbitrary classification, the small business plan may best be served without the added complication of semivariate cost.[53]
2. Analyze the prior years. Develop a "contribution margin" income statement, which splits the variable and fixed costs.
3. Project next year's costs. So long as there will be no radical change in operations, the planner can adjust and forecast.
4. Figure the marginal income ratio. This will be used to determine the amount of sales necessary to cover fixed costs and yield a target level of profit on a pretax basis.
5. Make a sales forecast. Look for attainable sales, determined on the basis of past experience, current business conditions, and the current level of net business assets in use.
6. Compare projected and actual performances. Before doing any comparison, sales for the year must be spread over a seasonal pattern. Monthly fixed-cost expenditures must also be established. When all revenues and expenses are combined, performance can be assessed.

This form of planning paves the way for the budgets and forecasts of an evolving firm. The smaller the organization, the fewer the budgets needed and the fewer the people involved. Regardless of the size of the operation, a written plan or formal budget can be of great assistance to those responsible for operations and finance in the small company.[54] At least three such "mini-budgets" are needed to encompass the activities of the firm: the capital budget, the operating budget, and the cash-flow budget. These relate very closely to the performance measures described at the beginning of this section.

A capital mini-budget is concerned with the traditional types of expenditures with a life longer than one year.[55] At the very least, a list should be drawn up showing the priorities of the assets and when they should be acquired. By adding cost to this list, a capital mini-budget can be produced. Ranking will help to further refine the process and allow the capital rationing that is often a part of small-business operation.

The second budget required is the operating budget. It is the accumulated estimates of operating revenues and expenses for the period. While traditional formulations of such a budget begin with a sales forecast, bottom-up approaches have been of demonstrable value.[56] By working upward from a desired profit toward a sales projection, the planner can gain better control over expenses by fixing the resources available to support different selling and manufacturing activity, then projecting the volume of sales that can be thus supported.

The final mini-budget is the cash budget, an estimate of the monetary flow in and out of the organization. This budget is the firm's most powerful tool in avoiding insolvency, and starts with basic information from the operating budget.[57] Next, this budget answers such questions as When supplier provides credit terms, when must invoices be paid? When are wages to be paid? When are other expected outflows to occur?

The total view expressed by critical measurements, and executive operational guide forecasting and mini-budgets may be sufficient for many firms. However, as they mature, businesses often find that events outpace their ability to explore alternatives. At some point, even smaller firms may be forced to develop computer-based planning and budgeting models.

Planning and Budgeting Systems

As the longer-term impact of present-day decisions is perceived, small firms will begin to implement strategic planning models.[58] The expansion decision will sometimes be the driving influence, although cash-flow and profit implications of proposed decisions will also motivate entrepreneurs.

For the small business, strategic models can take a form that recognizes the split between choices among alternatives (DSS) and the logic functions that build the financial planning model (PPM).[59] In the case of a modeling system built upon a matrix approach to data handling, such a system might hold actual, historical, base case and alternative choice data.[60] The PPM would contain data used to formulate the common pro-forma accounting statement, and be "driven" by a commonly available financial planning package, such as VisiCalc or SuperCalc on personal computers, or more sophisticated software on larger systems.

Most companies include a profit control function in their strategic planning package or model, which serves three functions.[61] First, it controls inputs to the accounting function, so that records can be complete and accurate. Second, it serves to reduce bookkeeping costs by automating the collection of much accounting data. Third, it maintains a complete financial data base that will yield a wealth of planning and control information.

The reader has now progressed through a sequence that has described the motivations, elements, and techniques of small-firm planning. While perspective has been gained, added focus may provide a better understanding of the costs and benefits of these activities for such economic units.

AN ASSESSMENT

A Means to an End

Many studies have concluded that small firms do not plan effectively. Few companies carry their efforts to anticipate sales and profit changes to the point of a formal plan of implementation. In fact, about all that can be said is that some small firms engage in "strategic thinking,"[62] which involves developing goals and objectives but does not include plans and programs for their achievement. The difficulty lies in the fact that planning is almost pure application, and often is not easily measurable until some time in the future.[63]

Since most small firms reflect the direction of their founder, they are entrepreneurial, and must rely upon this person to start the planning process.[64] Once this person's action shows benefit, others in the firm will follow suit and adopt a planning posture of their own. What must always be kept in mind is that the planning process, once begun, is no substitute for good decision making. Plans do not manage companies; people do. Planning must not be merely an intellectual exercise—attention must be paid to the substance and quality of effort.[65]

The objective of that effort is the effective use of resources in pursuit of attainable goals. It will yield dividends in many ways,[66] such as the following:

1. The ability to mobilize company resources, allocated to the most promising product lines and market areas, in accordance with predetermined goals and set priorities
2. Assisting the company to achieve those goals and objectives through planned and coordinated courses of action, with minimized duplication and waste
3. Developing more accurate short- and long-range forecasts, more balanced inventories, better production and materials programs, better budgets of capital funds, and improved use of human resources and plant facilities
4. The ability of management to concentrate on developing strategies and programs
5. Maintaining a competitive edge over other firms
6. Providing a basis for consistent and accurate measurement and comparison, which is vital if control is to be exercised.

Benefits and Costs

Specific user benefits can be identified for the small business that develops and uses a planning model. They are enhanced when such a model is computer-based, since this allows manipulation of more data faster. What "loss" occurs through a manual technique is limited to exploring fewer alternatives with longer turnaround.

Generally, the benefits are the following:[67]

1. Exploring more alternatives for price/volume/marketing, cost behavior, and other areas
2. Improved decision making; using projected cash-flow data to evaluate strategy impact, for instance
3. More confident decision-making; using better knowledge of short-term impact on revenue, cost, pricing, and volume

4. More effective planning; ability to replan quickly, test and reject alternatives, use of continuous budgeting
5. More timely information; nearly instantaneous for real-time systems, batch in days
6. Better understanding of the business, especially the impact of changes in variables subject to rational choice; all groups involved are "cross-sensitized" to the values of their different roles.

Costs of this type of planning are hard to measure. One can certainly measure it in terms of the time spent on this activity,[68] or the cost of computers and processing fees.[69] At the heart of the issue is the emotional change—the letting go of old habits. If this is a cost, then it must be paid if there is to be planning. For a firm to start modestly and not allow planning activity to take on a life of its own, the costs are not great—several thousand dollars over two years for a company having a $16 million in sales.[70] A smaller firm, using the aid of an agency or business school, might spend far less.

It must be stressed that such planning does bring real returns. In one study of 67 firms, systematic (strategic) planning led to increased sales, growing employment, and improved profitability. In addition, the lag time associated with these changes was brief.[71]

CONCLUSIONS

By now, it may be seen that strategic planning and budgeting are desirable and within the reach of even the smallest firm. It has been shown that planning does evolve over time as a result of growth of the firm and the infusion of more technologically advanced tools. With these thoughts in mind, the following recommendations about small-firm planning are made:

1. Scale the planning resources to the size of the firm, employing techniques described above
2. Whenever possible, use small business or personal computers to aid in data handling and faster turnaround
3. Share the effort of planning throughout the firm
4. To help assure a quick return on the effort, use bottom-up planning, shorter time horizons, and mini-budgets
5. As the firm grows, enrich the planning process.

If strategic planning is on target, it should provide the firm with a greater capacity for risk and a wider range of acceptable results.[72] In today's changing business environment, planning is not just desirable; it may very well be the way to survive.

NOTES

1. John A. Pearce, II, B. L. Chapman, and F. R. David, "Environmental Scanning for Small and Growing Firms," *Journal for Small Business Management,* July 1982, p. 30.

2. Donald L. Sexton and P. M. Van Auken, "Prevalence of Strategic Planning in Small Business, *Journal of Small Business Management,* July 1982, p. 35.

3. Ibid., p. 35.

4. Larry Green, "Planning and Decision Making in the Small Business," *Managerial Planning,* July/August 1982, p. 31.

5. Reed Moyer, "Strategic Planning for the Small Firm," *Journal of Small Business Management,* July 1982, p. 8.

6. Green, p. 27.

7. Pearce, Chapman, and David, p. 30.

8. Ibid.

9. John A. Welsh, and J. F. White, "A Small Business Is not a Little Big Business," *Harvard Business Review,* July–August 1981, p. 18.

10. Richard B. Robinson, Jr., and W. F. Littlejohn, "Important Contingencies in Small Firm Planning," *Journal of Small Business Management,* July 1981, p. 47.

11. Welsh and White, p. 18.

12. Ibid., p. 32.

13. Jacob Naor, "How to Make Strategic Planning Work for Small Business," *SAM Advanced Management Journal,* Winter 1980, p. 36.

14. W. David Jones, "Characteristics of Planning in Small Firms," *Journal of Small Business Management,* July 1982.

15. Ronald C. Clute, "How Important Is Accounting to Small Business Survival?" *The National Public Accountant,* June 1980, p. 27.

16. Moustafa H. Abdelsamad, "14 Financial Pitfalls for Small Business," *SAM Advanced Management Journal,* Spring 1977, p. 15.

17. Welsh and White, p. 26.

18. Clute, p. 28.

19. Abdelsamad, p. 20

20. Clute, p. 28.

21. Richard Robinson, "Forecasting and Small Business: A Study of the Strategic Planning Process," *Journal of Small Business Management,* July 1979, p. 21.

22. Clute, p. 27.

23. Arie Nagel, "Strategy Formulation for the Smaller Firm—A Practical Approach," *Long Range Planning,* August 1981, p. 119.

24. C. A. deKluyver and G. M. McNally, "Developing a Corporate Planning Model for a Small Company," *Long Range Planning,* February 1982, p. 97.

25. Robinson (1979), p. 20.

26. Ibid., p. 21.

27. George Rice and R. Hamilton, "Decision Theory and the Small Businessman," *American Journal of Small Business,* July 1979, p. 9.

28. Sexton and Van Auken, p. 21.

29. Green, p. 28.

30. Ibid., p. 29.

31. Moyer, p. 9.

32. William C. House, "Dynamic Planning for the Smaller Company—A Case History," *Long Range Planning,* July 1979, p. 43.

33. House, p. 41

34. Moyer, p. 11

35. Pearce, Chapman, and David, p. 31.

36. Moyer, p. 11.

37. Ibid., p. 12.

38. Ibid., p. 13.

39. House, p. 39.

40. Nagel, p. 116.

41. Stahrl W. Edmunds, "Performance Measures for Small Businesses," *Harvard Business Review*, January–February 1979, p. 172.

42. House, p. 48.

43. deKluyver and McNally, p. 99.

44. Roger L. Hayen, "Applying Decision Support Systems to Small Business Financial Planning," *Journal of Small Business Management*, July 1982, p. 35.

45. Ibid., p. 36.

46. Hui-Chuan Chen and R. C. Kick, Jr., "A Computer-Based Financial Management System for Small Business," *Management Adviser*, November–December 1973, p. 20.

47. Russell C. Kick, Jr., "A Profit Planning and Control System (PPCS) for the Small Firm," *Journal of Small Business Management*, October 1976, p. 8.

48. Edmunds, p. 173.

49. Ibid. An acceptable source of current data is the Robert Morris Associates *Annual Statement Studies*.

50. Ibid., p. 174.

51. Ibid., p. 176.

52. Donald Incrocci, "A Simplified Budget for Small Businesses," *The Practical Accountant*, May–June 1973, p. 43.

53. Ibid.

54. Jerry Prock, "Mini-Budgets: A Small Business Planning Tool," *Journal of Small Business Management*, December 1975, p. 12.

55. Ibid., p. 13.

56. John S. Chandler and T. N. Trone, "'Bottom-up' Budgeting and Control," *Management Accounting*, February 1982, p. 40.

57. Prock, p. 13.

58. deKluyver and McNally, p. 99.

59. Hayen, p. 37.

60. Chen and Kick, p. 21.

61. Kick, p. 13.

62. Sexton and Van Auken, p. 25.

63. Green, p. 29.

64. Ibid., p. 28.

65. House, p. 47.

66. Ibid., p. 46.

67. deKluyver and McNally, p. 105.

68. Robinson and Littlejohn, p. 45.

69. deKluyver and McNally, p. 106.

70. Ibid.

71. Robinson and Littlejohn, p. 47.

72. Green, p. 29.

Future Directions of Strategic Budgeting
——9——

We have now come to the point at which we must survey the future direction of strategic budgeting. As we have seen from both our study of the fundamentals and examples of applications, strategic budgeting is, and will continue to be, a necessity whenever we aim at more rigorous, shrewd, and creative resource application under conditions of uncertainty, turbulence, and discontinuity.

Particular emphasis should be placed on computerization, internationalization or globalization, and creative consolidation of strategic budgeting systems.

These seem to be the trends that will enhance the effectiveness and quality of strategic budgeting, regardless of the size of a firm. Each of these topics will be discussed below.

COMPUTERIZATION

In a broader sense, computerization can be understood within the framework of information systems, and may be more accurately represented as information-system-oriented strategic budgeting.

Although there are still absurd arguments that computerization will be of little help in strategic planning and management, it is beyond question that an intelligent use of information and computer systems is a basic requisite in strategic budgeting. As we get a better understanding of information systems and what they can accomplish in the future, the need to use them wisely in strategic planning and management will become clearer.

For example, if we join an international information access system and get access to international stock market information on an on-line basis, we will soon see that even if the U.S. stock markets are all bearish, we can almost always find a bullish market in some foreign country. The story is the same with the rise and fall in prices of strategic metals. By doing this, we will be able to get more pertinent information to determine what is feasible strategically than if we limit ourselves to domestic information.

It should be noted that the use of computers in strategic budgeting does not always involve modeling or simulation, but should encompass a wide variety of information collection, processing, analysis, retrieval, and evaluation. For example, as we develop a more sophisticated computer and communication network, we are more likely to get access to strategically applicable information. If we have to revise sales forecasts over the next five years, we will certainly want the forecasts from the five most trustworthy data base systems that offer estimates from various angles rather than from two systems.

Some of the systems may include the credibility of each estimate, and show on what assumptions and models the estimates are based. It will always be necessary to compare estimates of this sort with internally generated estimates, if internal estimates are prepared at the same time. It must be remembered that a highly reputable data base system does not always generate better estimates than one of ordinary quality. The assumptions, and the quality of the model on which the estimates are based, are most important, as far as forecast information is concerned.

With respect to information analysis and retrieval, we should become acquainted with the depth and scope of the computer-based services offered by data banks, service bureaus, and educational institutions.

For example, in 1979 the nationwide Telenet network offered access to 253 independent data bases and Telenet subscribers were offered 35 application programs in accounting and 39 in financial analysis. If we include not only general busines programs such as accounting, cash management, data base management, financial analysis, income tax computation, inventory control, job costing, message forecasting, project planning and control, pension management, photocomposition, professional time and cost, and records and text processing, but also engineering applications and scientific and technical applications, there are hundreds of application programs available.

Consequently, if our aim is to retrieve the best strategic information to build a strategic budget, we must continually review data bases to see which will be the best and most reliable. While such publications by Datapro, Auerbach, and Data Sources are of some help, we must not depend solely on their evaluations. Thus, tasks related to information retrieval should include selection of the base related to information evaluation.

These tasks include, first, identifying candidate bases and application programs and, if necessary, looking into the internal data bases and programs under construction. In some cases, we may need to use data bases, application programs, and all other services from external sources, while in others we may not have to use external systems, or at least not so extensively.

Second, evaluation of each data base, application program, and additional services, along with the direction of design and development of the strategic budgeting systems, should be continuous. This evaluation is not easy, and normally requires the services of a specialist in information systems to develop and evaluate the best strategic budgeting system tailored to the specific and overall needs of the corporation. Qualifications of such a professional will be discussed in the final section of this chapter.

Finally, the implementation and enhancement process should be undertaken after evaluation and development of the information systems, and budgetary planning and control.

The easiest areas in which to introduce computerization are computer-based strategic packages, as undertaken in decision packages in the zero-based budgeting system. The description of the nature of the package, goals, and action plans, intangible and tangible benefits and costs, consequences of nonapproval, cross-impacts of the package, and linkages to the specific strategic plan and contingency plan in Figure 4.3 can all be typed in, on an on-line or off-line basis. This will be in addition to rather brief information, such as quantitative benefit measures and tangible resources required, and the selection of appropriate items in the preliminary assessment summary.

The second easiest area will be computerizing a table of priority ranking, as shown in Figure 4.5. As soon as all strategic packages are submitted, shift the relevant information from each decision package to a table for preranking. If ranking of each strategic package is completed, a table of priority ranking is automatically generated. If the total budget figure has already been set, then upon prioritizing and accumulating all the figures of the strategic packages, an appropriate cutoff line can be established. In addition, multiple cutoff lines can be established, depending on the different funding levels set up.

A somewhat more difficult function to computerize is identification of the optimum ranking mixes, which are summarized in Table 4.5, and determination of the precise impact of one strategic package on others.

With respect to the former, regardless of the adoption of different ranking methods in a theoretical sense, it is most desirable to find a priority ranking that is stable and consistent. Therefore, a computer-based ranking analysis model has to output such tables as 4.3 and 4.4 as well as the results of ranking according to different approaches. In order to clarify the difference in value judgments, time-series ranking change, with or without use of the Delphi and related methods, may have to be developed.

Concerning the optimum ranking mixes, a table of multiple impacts is built by means of a computerized cross-impact model that can uncover possible interrelationships in terms of the intensity of direct and indirect effects of each strategic package on the others. This model may be adapted to strengthening established networks so that overlaps and redundancy can be held to a minimum.

As a natural development of information systems, the more difficult areas, such as creativity, innovation, and self-developing strategic budgeting systems, will start to be challenged toward the end of the 1980s by knowledge engineering and artificial intelligence.

Since many strategic thinking situations cannot be binary in nature, imprecise programming may become more important, so that a spectrum of situations can be dealt with in a more flexible manner. In the binary situation, even 80 percent right and 20 percent wrong means 100 percent right and 0 percent wrong, which tends to eliminate the possibility of flexibility. In addition, as more and more artificial intelligence is incorporated into the computerized information systems, natural language communication will be developed. If the responses of the computer in a query system enable the user to create new ideas and deeper insights, the system will be a great help in designing and developing creative strategic budgeting systems. As good systems accumulate, this will develop our own system and make it more useful for forecasting, sensitivity analysis, and optimizing the strategic budgeting system to the fullest extent.

INTERNATIONALIZATION

As long as American business continues to produce wherever the least expensive labor and the materials are available in the free world, and as long as a minimum quality of the product is maintained, internationalism will never diminish.

The essence of strategic budgeting is to achieve the most effective allocation of resources through as many organizations as possible on a global basis. This will be an important key to overcoming the traditional concepts of country and territory. In this case it implies more than internationalization, a term that does not include interdependence among countries.

As internationalization continues to develop in almost all areas of business, requirements in the strategic area, particularly strategic budgeting, should also increase.

The work of the Club of Rome, the Global Economic Model sponsored by the United Nations for bringing into focus international development strategy, and Project Link are three representative studies and models from which valuable inputs can be provided for strategic budgeting systems to help assess the future state of world economic development on a long-term basis.

They all seek to find out what must be done to achieve survival and growth. The Club of Rome warns that extrapolative efforts may endanger sustained economic growth and accelerated developments; they are political, social, and institutional in character, rather than physical. The Global Economic Model points out:

> To ensure accelerated development, two general conditions are necessary: first, far-reaching internal changes of a social, political and institutional character in the developing countries and second, significant change in the world economic order. Accelerated development leading to a substantial reduction of the income gap between the developing and the developed

countries can only be achieved through a combination of both these conditions. Clearly, each of them taken separately is insufficient, but when developed hand-in-hand, they will be able to produce the desired income.[1]

This statement is bolstered by an extensive input-output analysis made by Wassily Leontief, Nobel Prize laureate, and others. If it is valid, then policy formulation, strategic planning and budgeting should be the key concerns in both developing and developed countries.

If we are concerned with sound development in both the public and the private sectors among developed, developing, and less-developed countries, we will need to establish and maintain on a long-term basis a new international economic order that will include stabilization of commodity markets, stimulation of exports from developing countries, and means for increasing proper financing and smooth technological transfer. It is important for the companies in the United States to be aware of the significance of this direction of effort in the United Nations, OECD, and other international organizations. A desirable interaction pattern, and a suitable management philosophy and ideology of strategic budgeting that conform with these endeavors, must be developed.

The effort of Project Link is an attempt to analyze the economic effects of one country on the others by integrating econometric models or economic planning models developed by other countries under the supervision of Lawrence Klein, another Nobel Prize laureate. As the integration and analysis develop, it is anticipated that what should be done by both public and private sectors in each country to improve their economic development will be more clearly defined.

Even though a guideline or proposal has yet to emerge, the estimates provided by this kind of model will include economic information with many international ramifications. With the aid of the communications network, both scope and frequency of updating the information will be improved, and the usefulness of these outputs in internal and external strategic budgeting will be greatly improved.

The requirements of internationalization in the framework of strategic budgeting should be highly diversified. They must include the least expensive raw materials to be purchased and imported, the best location for establishing factories or the business headquarters, the best qualified labor force available, the best place for marketing and distribution, the best place for research and development, and the best place to sell or render services beyond the home country's national boundaries.

If the requirements above are not met, cooperative agreements among companies on an international basis will naturally proceed within the scope of legal requirements in each country. This sort of managerial, financial, or technological cooperative agreement will become more and more common toward the end of the 1980s.

This is one of the most important areas in which strategic budgeting should function. As illustrated briefly in the case of Apollo Industries in chapter 7, merger and acquisition issues are directly related to both long-term and short-term budgeting, in that we must consider the long-term effect of such options as they are affected by a change in the financial situation between the premerger and postmerger periods. In case of merger or acquisition, the perspective of strategic budgeting should not be biased, but should include all the other options as well, in order to strengthen the company.

Another important function of strategic budgeting is to establish a stronger linkage among market analysis, competitive margin, and budgeting, as illustrated in the case of Truck-Light in chapter 7. As the comparative and competitive market analyses become more advanced, the quality of strategic budgeting will improve because more key factors will be identified, and they will reflect more directly on the budgeting. Also, it is more likely that wasteful competition will be minimized by means of cooperative agreements with competitors on an international basis.

Still another important area will be the advancement of computerized strategic budgeting models and systems, as was partially illustrated in the case of Canon in chapter 7. The importance and use of these models and systems will be international in nature as external arrangements make possible the enhancement of international information-access systems.

By so doing, managerial and technological transfer will be further promoted and gaps filled in, to the extent that these activities are in conformity with the development of the company and that its investment capacity permits them. The success or failure of internationalization toward the end of the 1980s will, therefore, be in part due to the internal motivation, evolution, and development of the organization, and in part due to formation of a pertinent policy in the public sector and constant interaction between public and private sectors to enhance international socioeconomic and technological development.

TOWARD A CONSOLIDATED STRATEGIC BUDGETING SYSTEM

The core concept of strategic budgeting has been insightful resource allocation by means of systematic linkage and consolidation, or integration. Consolidation means, in essence, an effort to minimize redundancy or duplication in order to increase the overall effectiveness of the system—that is, the strategic budgeting system.

It also connotes finding out the important ingredients (the minimum possible number) of the system. As shown in Figure 2.3, the basic dichotomy of a strategic budgeting system can be a strategic planning system and a comprehensive budgeting system.

However, such integrated strategic planning and budgeting—that is, a strategic budgeting system—that may be an outgrowth of international marketing, econometrics, accounting, financial planning, research and development, and zero-based budgeting systems may not alone be able to satisfy the future requirements for a strategic budgeting system.

In addition to a strategic budgeting system we need to design and develop the assessment system on the basis of legislative change, on both a domestic and international basis, on the basis of a human development distribution system, and on the basis of a strategic budgeting evaluation system.

Since changes in legal requirements require substantial changes in strategic budgeting, we need to be able to retrieve all the new laws and changes in established laws that can have grave effects on our strategic planning and budgeting. By the time the law takes effect, the impact study must be completed and a revised strategic budget established. The introduction of on-line information systems and some sort of computer conference system will be necessary to keep up with the transitions and take the necessary strategic action.

Even at the cost of paying less attention to other key functions, the importance of a human development distribution system cannot be overlooked. People of exceptional competence are needed to develop the strategic budgeting system. They should have the ability to read the core stream in the foreseeable future, as well as the ability to integrate seemingly impossibly diversified components into an orderly system. The effect of synergy must be thoroughly understood and applied, whenever necessary.

Certainly, a broad knowledge of budgeting as well as of strategic planning and management, bolstered by technological and legal knowledge, is the prerequisite; this, plus a successful record, should be proof of piercing insight, profound logic, and a firm belief in the importance of strategic budgeting. It is imperative for us to explore what sort of education and training can best produce personnel with these qualifications.

At no other period have we felt the need as much as we do now for the services of innovative and brilliant people who can revitalize the present state of the world's socioeconomy. This "new breed" should understand how to convert energy wasted in confrontation to energy saved in harmony, and suspicion to trust. Knowledge and skills will be wasted unless we can find an educational approach to do these things.

The evolution and development of strategic budgeting will never be complete without establishment of an appropriate strategic budgeting evaluation, and the taking of appropriate action. Evaluation criteria can be established on the basis of timing, productivity, and net benefit as a result of employing the strategic budgeting system.

Timing means not only overall timing but also timing appropriate to the generation of each specific report and information need. Timing requirements can be specified in each case of the program, or project, and they are compared with the actual timing to discover the information generation and distribution capabilities of the system. If a subsystem detrimental to timing is identified, then the reason is determined and remedial action is taken to strengthen the linkage and integration of the subsystem to the overall strategic budgeting system. As cases accumulate, it is quite probable that more redundancies and duplications will be eliminated.

Productivity is another criterion to be established. This is a measure of the extent to which the required information is produced within a given time. For an information user, it is the rate of satisfaction of information requirements. Even if information has been gathered in the required period, it is without value if it does not meet either overall or specific requirements.

In strategic budgeting, productivity is by no means limited to the number of pages of budgeting reports produced in a given time, but must include the increase in the quality of the information, and its value when distributed to the right persons in time for effective use.

The quality of information should be a constant issue, to be resolved before the end of the 1980s. Every effort should be made to improve it, and its pertinence to the task of increasing productivity.

We will need to approach this problem from at least three different perspectives. One is from the human side, by establishing and augmenting at the outset the number of criteria for information, such as accessibility, comprehensiveness, applicability, accuracy, appropriateness, clarity, flexibility, verifiability, freedom from bias, quantifiability, predictability, and suggestibility. Each criterion must be clearly defined in the light of the objectives and scope of strategic budgeting, and its relative importance must be clarified.

These criteria may not need to be applied equally to all aspects of budgeting, and we will have to develop specific applications for each, depending on the nature of the implementation and enhancement issues of budgeting. Care must be taken when developing overall and specific criteria that, first, they are truly relevant to the task of increasing the quality of information and, second, that we can ascertain, through the use of these criteria, the increase in the quality of the information and, hence, the increase in productivity in the information service.

Another approach is from the machine side, and involves the use of the available hardware to increase the quality of information. For example, with the development of word-processing systems, users have a greater opportunity to revise and implement the contents of the information on an on-line basis. The more ways we have of correcting and revising information at any given time, the more likely it is that we can significantly enhance the quality of the information.

One way to enhance the quality of information is by the use of graphic displays in color, aided by language information. This will often greatly increase the level of comprehension. The criteria of the implementation of strategic budgeting can be stored and retrieved whenever necessary for further revision and exploration.

It will not be possible to improve the quality of information without integrating both human and machine efforts, and an appropriate balance between them will be called for. In this area, continuous management of hardware, at the highest level of expertise, should be constantly investigated.

At one extreme, the integrative issues of international strategic budgeting can be related to the resource allocation of nuclear weapons—that is, how many nuclear weapons should be produced and deployed at land and sea bases, assessing the intensity of the threats—and at the other extreme, to an individual who has international resources.

If the decision of the present government is to increase the defense budget more than investment in private sectors, more companies will shift to military products and their strategy will have to be integrated with markets of a different nature. One noteworthy difference between military and nonmilitary markets is that military markets do not exist except when competitive bidding is required on the part of entry participants. Nonmilitary markets require constant marketing, research and developments, and product changes in a sharper competitive environment.

When operating in a military market, two factors must be kept in mind in the process of strategic planning and budgeting: How long we plan to produce these military products, and, upon completion of the present contract, whether we can beneficially convert to nonmilitary products.

All other integrative issues that might arise at the extreme end of international strategic budgeting would result from globalization. Within the framework of international accounting, it may mean that we must take every possible advantage of financial and managerial accounting principles and practices, because principles may not be the same from one country to another.

For example, after looking at foreign-currency transfer methods, we see that the monetary-nonmonetary method adopted by Australia, New Zealand, and Mexico is different from the current-noncurrent method used by Canada, Pakistan, and Bermuda, and that both these methods are different from the current-rate method adopted by a majority of enterprises in Denmark, France, Japan, the Netherlands, Norway, and the United Kingdom.

The method you adopt may change the amount of gain or loss in the transaction substantially, ranging from $300 million dollars loss in exchange to $400 million gain, based on the table of Choi and Mueller.[2]

Another example can be drawn from the statutory tax rates in various countries. According to *Foreign and U.S. Corporate Income and Withholding Tax Rates*, published by Ernst and Ernst in 1977, the statutory profit tax rate in Iran was 13.4 percent, and in Libya, 60.0 percent, approximately 4.5 times as

FIGURE 9.1. Desirable directions of integrated strategic budgeting.

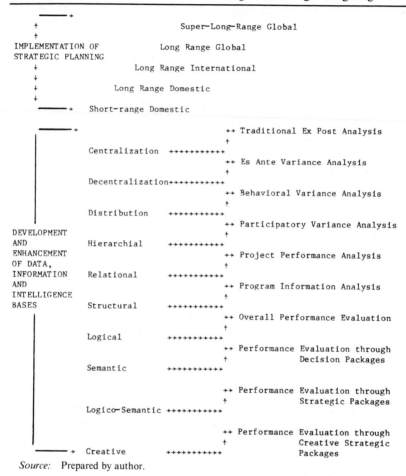

Source: Prepared by author.

much. The same applied to the dividend withholding rate, ranging from 0 percent in the United Kingdom, Lebanon, and Saudi Arabia to 60 percent in Iran. It is vitally important to examine the differences in accounting standards, principles, and practices between countries.

Large accounting firms with branches in foreign countries have been continuously checking the accounting methods and practices in these nations. *Financial Accounting Principles—A Survey in 46 Countries*, published by Price Waterhouse and Company International, will be particularly helpful in looking up the details. Another report, *Professional Accounting in 30 Countries*, published by the American Institute of Certified Public Accountants, will also be of great help in understanding the U.S. professional viewpoints.

Thus, we must be alert to strategic budgeting as related to political thrust in the present administration and the next one, and to the movement of international accounting developments, in order to discern the fruitfulness of long-term international investment.

On the basis of the above, we can now portray the desired direction of integrated strategic budgeting in terms of longer-range global scope with regard for the harmonious development of all nations. This will be carried out by the optimum allocation of limited resources among less-developed, developing, and developed countries, and the use of more creative data, information, intelligence, and integrative performance evaluation through means of creative strategic packages, as shown in Figure 9.1.

The more we are concerned with a desirable balance among global international and domestic allocation of resources to achieve sound growth for the benefit of all people, the more likely it is that we will increase the quality of life as well as human survival. This should be the ultimate objective of strategic budgeting.

NOTES

1. Wassily Leontief, Anne F. Carter, and Peter A. Petri, *The Future of World Economy* (New York: Oxford University Press, 1977), p. 11.

2. See D. S. Choi and Gerhard G. Mueller, *An Introduction to Multinational Accounting* (Englewood Cliffs, N. J.: Prentice-Hall, 1978), Table 3–3, p. 73.

Epilogue

—10—

IMPLICATIONS OF STRATEGIC BUDGETING

Regardless of our interests, a resource allocation resulting from strategic planning determines the future of a person, an organization, a country, or even the world.

Particularly in the sphere of military strategic planning in the United States and the Soviet Union, breaking the equilibrium as a result of one side's assuming that the retaliatory attack will not be so devastating that shelters cannot cope with it, and making a preemptive attack, would you have devastating results.

Under such circumstances, where both sides have more than 15,000 warheads attachable to submarine-launched ballistic missiles or ICBMs, more than 10,000 targets, civilian or miitary, would be destroyed, even assuming only 70 percent penetration. Since the United States has from 1 to 30 army, navy, or air force bases in each state, as well as 1,600 underwater-based ballistic missiles, there are still enough missiles left for nonmilitary targets, such as military-industrial zones mixed with nonmilitary ones, and large, medium, and small cities.

According to the final figures of the 1970 census, there are approximately 3,900 locations with 6,200 or more inhabitants; estimating conservatively, the balance of the towns with 15,000 inhabitants would become targets.

To make matters worse, the resulting atmospheric contamination would cause darkness in the daytime and agriculture would collapse. Survivors would probably starve. Sir Douglas Black, speaking as a physician, predicts that while there would be many casualties in the event of a nuclear attack, there would also be millions of survivors, but they could not be fed or cared for.[1]

A basic question frequently raised is, "Is the number of nuclear weapons sufficient to be a deterrant to anyone contemplating a first strike?" Even a brief calculation reveals the irrational and disastrous outcome of such a course, and normal leaders of countries will not opt for it. The best course of action in this situation is to avoid the pattern of continually increasing tension between nations, so as to avoid circumstances that produce abnormal decisions.

In other words, allocate resources away from areas saturated with nuclear games and into more healthy and productive channels for the welfare and improvement of mankind. This is the most important issue in strategic budgeting on a long-term international basis. We should develop cooperative long-term projects extending across national boundaries by mutually compensating for strengths and weaknesses in such areas as space exploration, exploitation of the seabed, robotics, artificial intelligence, and synthetic foods.

Furthermore, super-large-scale projects can be undertaken by an international task force in such areas as nullifying or mitigating the effects of hurricanes, typhoons, or cyclones, preventing famine or floods, and increasing food supplies in countries where thousands starve and many more are hungry.

The impetus for programs such as these should come from suggestions made at summit meetings and in the General Assembly of the United Nations and other appropriate organizations after they have seriously considered these issues. Then, there should be meetings involving the public and private sectors, including the discussions of working groups aimed at identifying, say, the top 20 projects to be undertaken and completed toward the end of the twentieth century.

This program could be termed World New Deal, as an extension on an international scale of the economic policies carried out by Presidents Roosevelt and Truman. The increased role of the private sector, however, will differentiate it from the classic program illustrated by the historic New Deal. Each company, multinational or national, must be given freer opportunity to seek (or become) a sister company in an appropriate corporate venture, the extent and type of which will be subject to the individual requirements of the company.

Most important is the full support of the government of each company's country. The criteria for support of these projects should be based on global evolution and survival rather than national interest. While completely ignoring the national interest is impractical, the important world leaders must be committed to placing global evolution ahead of national interest. Without full awareness of the importance of this policy by all nations, the new world revitalization policy cannot be put into effect.

If this kind of arrangement can be made, strategic thinking and budgeting will prevail among highly developed countries, the developing ones, and the less-developed. Thus the directions required, the projects to be undertaken, the incentives needed for cooperation, and the resource allocations will all be clarified.

Leadership from the top down, however, must be supported by internal participation throughout, typified by such activities as quality control circles now common in the United States and Japan.

PARTICIPATORY FORMULATION OF STRATEGIC BUDGETING

Like zero-based budgeting, strategic budgeting is participatory in nature. However, requirements for participation in strategic budgeting, in its final form, are on a much larger scale and are global in nature.

In our previous example, nuclear arms limitation, progress may be made as a result of the voices of hundreds of thousands of people all over the earth, disregarding national boundaries, being heard and acted upon by top officials of the United States and the Soviet Union.

The more skillful the people of the community become in demonstrating the preferences of the majority, the more likely it becomes that these preferences will be acted upon in the political arena. It is not out of the question that an electronic voting system could revive the method of referendum, through which the participation of all the people, rather than of representatives, is the activating factor. In other words, in both the public and private sectors, the constituency would be able to participate directly in solutions for the long-term, important issues as well as in short term, less important ones.

In the corporate sphere, every employee can be given an opportunity to get involved in important strategic budgeting issues. If each employee has a chance to vote on such issues, the clear implication is that he or she understands the issues and, as a result of voting, will be more positively motivated to implement and enhance the development of the system on which he or she voted.

Since we must realize that such total participation is still an ideal, not a reality, we must search for and consider other, more realistic methods of participation.

One of the best methods is to establish a core, or nucleus, person for the design and development of a participatory system. The core person may be a strategic (budgetary) unit manager or a group manager. Second, the core person designs the scope and depth of participation by the subordinates as well as upper-echelon managers. Feedback and feedforward of the strategic budgeting information to and from the core person will reinforce participation by all persons concerned.

The particular ability needed by the core person is insight that enables him or her to visualize the kind and style of participation by each person that will best meet the basic and applied strategic budgeting information requirements of the company. A clear distinction must be made between those who provide information, those who process and integrate information, and those who review information.

Ordinarily, in the process of analyzing the macro environment, while the economists and environment specialists become information providers, the core person and group become receivers of information from which opportunities and threats, strengths and weaknesses, and the priorities of strategic thrusts will be formulated. It should be noted that, depending on the extent and effectiveness of the participation, minor or even serious gaps may be discovered between what should be and what can be done.

More concretely, if effective communications are developed through an adequate method of participation, there will arise a much deeper understanding of the premises of the economic and environmental forecasts, in addition to other sources of information, so that it will be much easier to determine whether the differences between what can and should be done are surmountable. It is by no means satisfactory to depend on written documents or reports, which may be nothing more than general statements and may not even relate to the specific environment that may have great impact on the development of a specific line by a specific company.

Third, on the basis of the system established, a concrete schedule of participatory action by groups, members of groups, and each person should be formulated and organized, as shown in Figure 10.1. This kind of figure should result from internal determination among all the personnel involved. The utmost care must be taken to assure that participation is not provided and framed from the top, but created by the participants.

Fourth, the established schedule should be carried out. What is important for the core person at this stage is to avoid involving himself or herself too deeply in the established schedule and process. The core person needs to be able to look at matters objectively, in order to judge which aspects of the participation plan are unproductive, or too time-consuming to be retained for future implementation and enhancement. In a smaller organization, the participation system can be carried out more easily because there are fewer participants.

The productivity of the participation may be evaluated by a number of criteria, among which are the number of new ideas or suggestions generated within a given time, a concise yet in-depth response to the questions raised, the number of hidden issues uncovered, and the number of priority decisions made in a given time. In many conferences, saturation and repetition of ideas already developed are most frequent. The core person as chairman, or even as participant, at a meeting should understand the symptoms of saturation and be aware of the point of diminishing returns so that an appropriate break can be taken, and another meeting set up. When generating new ideas is of the utmost importance, it is particularly helpful to change the place and environment of these meetings.

TOWARD FEEDFORWARD CONTROL AND AUTOPOIESIS[2]

Just as the nervous sytem of a human develops and senses provide a variety of possible responses as one grows older, a strategic budgeting system evolves.

FIGURE 10.1. Participatory strategic planning and budgeting cycle, industrial products manufacturer.

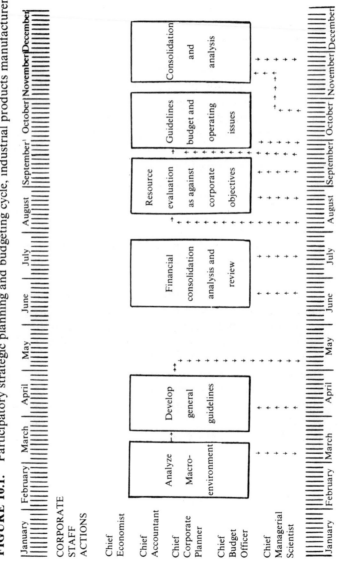

212

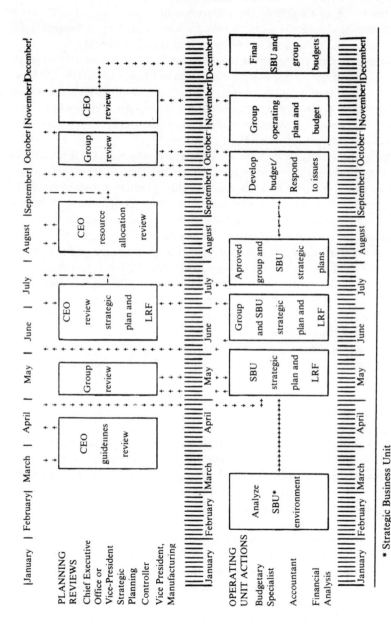

* Strategic Business Unit

Source: Rochelle O'Connor, "Resource Allocation and Strategic Planning," The Conference Board, *Information Bulletin* no. 99, 1981, p. 5.

Feedback mechanisms should be carefully installed so that the planned and actual performances may be measured accurately and compared, and remedial action, if required, can be taken by the appropriate personnel without undue delay. The actions should be planned to meet the objectives rather than simply to nullify the difference between planned and actual performance. If the gap is large, it may be wise to narrow it by successive actions, rather than planning to eliminate it at the next period.

However perfect the feedback mechanism incorporated into the strategic budget may be, the strategic budgeting system can never be perfect if it lacks feedforward and self-organizing functions. To put it another way, the system needs both early sensing or preempting and learning-from-failure functions. The former is creative, forward-looking, and forward-cognitive, whereas the latter is adjustable, adaptive, and self-repairing.

The two functions are evolutionary in nature, which makes it possible to enhance the quality of strategic budgeting systems. The feedforward function reinforces the system to make it more highly predictive and sensitive to unforeseen circumstances and incidents. The ultimate effect of the function should be regarded as creating the art of possibles—that is, what should be the most reasonable outcome on the basis of the information given. The more we study and experience the creative aspect of strategic planning and budgeting, the more likely it is that we will be able to employ the feedforward function effectively. Ackoff says that inquiries into the nature of creativity and development of creativity enhancement procedures should be integrated.[3] What is crucial, however, is the lack of a relevant theory through which the integrated result may be further explored.

Until such a theory is available, we must employ such procedures for enhancing creativity as synectics, brainstorming, AKJ (Approach by Kawaleita Jiro), the search conference, the dialectical approach, and idealized design. The work done on the nature of creativity has been predominantly descriptive and does not specify the relevant type of practice, which is what we need most.

The self-organization function is internal in nature, and the core can be considered as the mind and spirit of the participants, particularly in regard to cooperation and coordination. If these are lacking or not exercised to the fullest, even the best-planned strategic budgeting system will fail. This function, too, will evolve slowly and steadily, but once matured, it becomes one of the most important factors in the success of any strategic budgeting system, no matter what else may happen.

From another point of view, the self-organizing function is a continuous mechanism through which repeated errors can be minimized or totally eliminated. With this function in full effect, the system can better cope with difficulties because more options are open. For example, if a strategic budgeting system is highly self-organizing, it is highly likely that weaknesses of one strategic planning unit will be compensated for by the strengths of another up to the point where the strategic planning unit can function independently, or can be equipped with the means of strengthening itself if it is attacked by competitors.

The essence of the self-reorganization process is the changing of weaknesses to strengths by diagnosing the external threats and utilizing internal remedies. If enough remedies are available, there is no problem in coping with ordinary threats. If the threat is formidable, special remedies will be required. Under such circumstances the self-discipline of constituents of the system may be the key to whether it can cope with the extraordinary threat.

The power of self-organization is represented by the integration of mind, spirit, motives, and aspirations of the constituents of the strategic budgeting system. The longer they have been functioning in an evolving manner, the stronger this power becomes, and beyond a certain limit of self-organization, no one can compete with it.

Successful strategic budgeting should come from such self-organization or autopoiesis, bolstered by a cybernetic amalgamation between feedback and feedforward control systems.

NOTES

1. *New York Times*, April 4, 1982, p. 15. It is said that total armament costs in 1981 reached $500 billion in the world, and 1 million atomic bombs equivalent to the Hiroshima type are now available. This equals three tons of TNT for every person in the world.

2. On autopoiesis, see W. Ross Ashby, "Principles of the Self-Organizing Dynamic System," *Journal of General Psychology* 37 (1947): 125–28; Erich Jantsch, ed., *The Self-Organizing Paradigm of Evolution* (New York: Pergamon, 1980); Milan Aeleny, ed., *Autopoiesis: A Theory of the Living Organization* (New York: North Holland, 1981).

3. For more discussion, see R. L. Ackoff and E. Vergara, "Creativity in Problem Solving and Planning: A Review," *European Journal of Operations Research* 7 (1981): 1-14.

Index

About the Author

Professor Akira Ishikawa was born in Odawara City, Japan in 1934. His interests lie in Business and Public Administration, Accounting and Management Information, and Systems. He obtained his MA at the University of Washington in 1969, then studied at the University of Texas, where he received a PhD in 1972. He did post–doctoral studies at Massachusetts Institute of Technology in 1973. He taught at New York University, Graduate School of Business Administration, 1972-76. In 1977 he was appointed Visiting Professor at the University of Hawaii, and has since held similar posts at: Yokohama City University, Japan, 1979-80; Aoyama Gakuin University, Japan, 1979-80; and Rissho University Japan, 1979-81. The editor of "Planning and Control," published in 1974, he has written and had published "Corporate Planning and Control Model Systems," 1975 and "Zero-Base Budgeting for Implementing Management Effectiveness," 1978. Professor Ishikawa was awarded a grant from IBM (Japan) for holding the First International Symposium on Zero-Base Planning and Budgeting, and also received grants from the Commemorative Association for the Japan World Exposition, National Institute for Research Advancement, Japan Productivity Centre. He also received a Merit Award from the Marquis Who's Who Publications Board in the USA. The Programme Director of TIMS 22nd International Conference, he co-chaired both the US-Japan Conference on Product Development which was sponsored by the Ministry of International Trade and Industry, and the First International Symposium on Zero-Base Planning and Budgeting. Professor Ishikawa is a member of the Japan Society Incorporated, American Accounting Association, American Society for Cybernetics, International Federation of Information Processing Societies, and International Federation of Operations Research Societies. His biography appears in "Who's Who in the East," "Men of Achievement," and "Dictionary of International Biography." He is an Advisor to The United States Congressional Advisory Board, Research Advisor to The Institute for Advanced Studies, Walden University, and a Professor of International Politics, Economics and Business Administration, Aoyama Gakuin University.